THE LAST LINE OF DEFENSE

The LAST LINE OF DEFENSE

How to Beat the Left in Court

ERIC SCHMITT

BROADSIDE BOOKS

HarperCollins books may be purchased for educational, business, or sales promotional use. For information, please email the Special Markets Department at SPsales@harpercollins.com.

hc.com

FIRST EDITION

Library of Congress Cataloging-in-Publication Data
Names: Schmitt, Eric Stephen, 1975– author.
Title: The last line of defense : how to beat the Left in court / Eric Schmitt.
Description: New York: Broadside Books, 2025.
Identifiers: LCCN 2025016753 | ISBN 9780063437180 (hardcover) | ISBN 9780063437197 (ebook)
Subjects: LCSH: Law—Missouri—History. | Courts—Missouri—History. | Courts—United States. | Legislation—United States. | Attorneys General—Missouri. | Missouri. Attorney General's Office. | Right and left (Political science)
Classification: LCC KFM7878 .S36 2025 | DDC 349.77809/052—dc23/eng/20250521
LC record available at https://lccn.loc.gov/2025016753

25 26 27 28 29 LBC 5 4 3 2 1

To my family

The Party told you to reject the evidence of your eyes and ears. It was their final, most essential command.

—George Orwell, *1984*

CONTENTS

INTRODUCTION

In November 2024, the fever broke.

The American people decided to reject the excesses of the Biden-Harris Administration. Nearly every region, every state, every demographic group became redder. Athletes confidently wore MAGA hats, frat guys posted videos with "YMCA" blaring in the background, Miss America sported a "Make America Healthy Again" dress, and the Trump dance swept through social media. The vibe shift was undeniable. America was back.

As I write this in early 2025, President Donald Trump is fulfilling the mandate given to him by the American people. He has reversed the Biden Administration's executive orders on climate extremism, immigration, and the dangerous racialization of American life. Major banks are backing away from ESG policies, corporations are abandoning DEI agendas, and even Mark Zuckerberg has admitted to Meta's censorship efforts under Biden. In fact, I sat not too far from that same Mark Zuckerberg on January 20, 2025, in the Capitol Rotunda as President Trump delivered his stirring second inaugural address—the culmination of the greatest political comeback in American history. A new Golden Age for America seemed within reach.

As we look back on the past few years and the long night before the fever broke, we might be tempted to believe that this outcome was inevitable. Given how badly the Biden Administration screwed things up—and how sloppily conceived so many of Joe Biden's policy objectives and executive actions were—it might seem that The Left's agenda was destined for failure.

But as we hop in that time machine for just a moment, it's important to remember just how much of a hold the woke Left had over this country for the four-year period preceding Inauguration Day 2025. It was a time that included mandatory lockdowns, compulsory Covid shots, deliberately open borders, DEI struggle sessions, ESG requirements, and a censorship enterprise so vast that it stands as the greatest assault on the First Amendment in the history of the United States. It's no wonder they're attempting to make us forget all about it today. Back then, with President Trump and his allies out of power, it fell mostly to relatively unknown individuals to fight the good fight, hold back the onslaught in the darkest days, and be the last line of defense.

As it happened, I had been the Attorney General of Missouri for just over two years when the Biden Administration took office. No one in my family was a lawyer. I didn't know any lawyers growing up. But I was attracted to the law because it gave structure and protection for regular folks to live their lives and pursue happiness, whatever that meant for them. In courtrooms, the rules still matter. Before judges and juries, lawyers can marshal facts and reveal the truth. During the tail end of the Trump Administration, my office had focused primarily on fighting crime and keeping our streets safe. When the left-wing lunatics of the Biden Administration took office, everything changed. We added another mission: holding the line and pushing back against the most radical Administration in modern political history.

This wasn't an easy fight. There were times when it seemed hopeless and even lonely. But we prevailed on many of the issues that mattered most to the American people. Primarily, we did this through the American legal system, which operates on cold logic and hard facts. Whenever the Biden Administration signed a new executive order or put out some obscure rule change, my team would challenge it in court, getting injunctions while we fought the battles that needed fighting. We stopped mask mandates for millions of people. We prevented millions more from being fired simply for refusing to take the Covid-19 shot. We fought back against Biden's war on American energy and we started the legal investigations that ultimately helped lead to the demise of ESG and Net-Zero policies. Later, we stopped the Biden Administration's blatantly illegal attempts to cancel student loan debt, and we held off and helped reduce the flow of illegal immigration (at least for a while) using all the legal tools at our disposal. Many of the cases we brought are still working their way through the court system or have established important precedent for the fights yet to come. One of them, *Missouri v. Biden* (later referred to as *Murthy v. Missouri*), revealed key information about the Biden Administration's unlawful pressure campaign on Meta, YouTube, Twitter, and other tech platforms to suppress speech, laying the groundwork for the free speech revolution and renaissance we are seeing today.

By the time this book is published, the Left will undoubtedly be expanding their fight with the Trump Administration. Democrat AGs from across the country continue to challenge the President's executive orders and policies in court, just as my colleagues and I did with the Biden Administration. But there are key differences between their efforts and ours. Our lawsuits sought to restore individual liberty, defend the rule of law, fight for everyday Americans against the massive power of the federal government, and prevent government overreach. In contrast, Democrat lawsuits aim to preserve the expansion of government power at the *expense* of individual freedom and the rule of law. Right now, they are fighting to defend the unchecked power of the Left-captured government bureaucracy to defy the will of the American people. They are fighting to keep Biden's regulations and practices—regulations and practices that no one ever voted on—in place. And they will work to block President Trump's efforts to protect the country.

We also had the law—and common sense—on our side. We did then, and we do now. President Trump emphasized this in his second inaugural address when he spoke about restoring the rule of common sense. The policies we challenged under Biden were radical, and American voters would never have approved them in a straight up-or-down vote: the reckless green agenda, open-border policies, secretive government censorship programs, and tyrannical mask and vaccine mandates. These initiatives contradicted fundamental American values.

By contrast, the policies the Left and their judicial allies are now attacking—securing the border, restoring energy independence, eliminating waste, and defending free speech—are deeply popular with the American people. Our legal battles were the polar opposite of the Left's current campaign. We fought to uphold America's core values against an onslaught from the radical Left, while they now seek to use activist judges to undermine those values (and Biden did install more than two hundred more of them during his term). The players may have changed, but the principles at stake remain the same.

Moreover, President Trump and his team are prepared for the fight. Their four-year hiatus sharpened their focus and strategy. This White House is free of many of the more establishment figures who once slowed progress. For four years out of power, the President worked with brilliant conservative policy experts to craft executive orders and policies designed to withstand even the fiercest legal challenges. These initiatives address real needs and injustices. President Trump and his team are committed to fulfilling campaign promises and winning the argument with the American people.

The Left, especially during the disastrous Biden-Harris years, worked differently. Biden and his radical bunch forced policies on the American people regardless of their legality. Biden even admitted, at times, that if courts deemed his actions illegal, he would find a way to do it anyway. As *The Wall Street Journal* put it, "Mr. Biden said his original plan to 'provide millions of working families with debt relief for their college student debt' was derailed by 'MAGA Republicans' and 'special interests' who challenged the plan in court. 'The Supreme Court blocked it,' Mr. Biden added, 'but that didn't stop me.'" Biden—or, more accurately, the people propping him up—believed they could exploit a series of manufactured "emergencies" to bypass the law. The Covid-19 pandemic became a never-ending "crisis" or "emergency" even when case counts for everyone, including the most vulnerable, were way down. Student debt was an "emergency." Climate change and the so-called assault on "trans rights" were "emergencies." These labels gave them cover to bend or arguably break the law with sloppy executive orders that were extremely vulnerable to legal challenges.

Today—and thankfully, by the way—the "zombie cases" that the Biden Administration resuscitated in an attempt to stop President Trump from running again, to bankrupt him and his family and put him in jail for the rest of his life, are gone. The executive orders that Joe Biden enacted with the stroke of a pen have all been undone with another stroke of a pen, showing the dangers presented by the Biden team. As I continue my work as a United States Senator, I am prouder than ever of the work my small team and I did to hold the line against these unprecedented attacks by the Left against our Constitution, our individual liberties, and our way of life. We were on the front line of freedom and the last line of defense until President Trump could return to the White House.

I also believe it's worth remembering just how egregiously the Democrat Party behaved when *they* were the ones in power. As we go forward, I'm sure many leaders in that party will pretend they don't remember. They won't want to talk about the Covid lockdowns, the mask mandates, or all the ways that the Biden Administration's actions flew directly in the face of the American legal system. Of course, by now virtually all discussion of President Biden's preemptive pardons (presumably signed by autopen) for Anthony Fauci,

Mark Milley, and several members of his family has disappeared from the news cycle.

But I haven't forgotten. And I don't think you should either. As the Czech writer Milan Kundera once wrote, "The struggle of man against power is the struggle of memory against forgetting." Maintaining our constitutional republic, defending our freedoms, and protecting this great American experiment depends on learning lessons from our past—especially recent lessons about a descent into petty totalitarianism. So, with that in mind, let's strap on our masks, sanitize our hands, wipe down our grocery bags, socially distance, sidestep the playground police tape, and look over our shoulders for Covid Karens.

For the first few chapters of this book, we are taking the Delorean back in time to the very first hours of the Covid-19 pandemic.

Part I

The Covid Wars

Chapter 1

ATTACK OF THE "EXPERTS"

We all remember the first sign that something was wrong. For me, it came during a meeting of the Republican Attorneys General Association (RAGA) in Washington, D.C., held in early March 2020. Looking out at the crowds during one of the early meetings, I noticed that they were smaller. Many companies had instituted travel restrictions and so their folks were not in attendance. Talking to a few of the other attendees, I learned that many people had canceled their flights for fear of contracting the new disease or virus or whatever it was. The chatter about this mysterious ailment toward the end of the conference reached a fevered pitch. But what was it?

"It's like the flu," someone told me, staring up at a television in the corner that was playing cable news. "I guess they're calling it the 'novel coronavirus.'" A few minutes later, someone else said bodies were stacking up in China.

What? I thought.

At first I didn't think much of it. By then I'd lived through a few public panics over new diseases that ultimately turned out to be far less severe than the news pundits predicted. Back in 2009, when I was beginning my tenure in the Missouri Senate, everyone was talking about "swine flu," a supposedly deadly strain of influenza that we were told would sweep through the population. Somehow we managed to handle that without triggering a global pandemic. A few years later, we heard similar warnings about a potential Ebola outbreak that never quite materialized. Rather than panic, I decided to keep my focus and go about my work. It had my attention, sure, but we had a job to do. That was, of course, until it felt like the world came to a stop.

In January 2019, I was sworn in as Missouri's forty-third Attorney General. In that first year, before the virus upended everything in 2020, my primary goal was fighting crime and keeping Missourians safe. In early 2019 we launched the Safer Streets Initiative, a groundbreaking program that deputized assistant AGs in my office as assistant U.S. Attorneys to prosecute violent crimes. We invested significant resources into finding and testing sexual assault kits, some of which had been gathering dust on office shelves for many years. Then, in January 2020, I personally prosecuted a murder case in St. Louis—a high-stakes move that put an exclamation point on my first year in office.

So, we were rolling when the world shut down.

I remember watching some college basketball with some longtime friends in a house on Clay Street in Jefferson City and learning that some NBA games had been canceled. Players were concerned about the same things we had been hearing about a few weeks earlier at the RAGA conference. They didn't want to get on planes or be in close proximity to one another. They didn't know enough about this new virus to risk traveling. Within hours, the entire rest of the NBA season had been scrapped. Then it was other sports, concerts, flights, and long-planned family reunions. Restaurants in my hometown of St. Louis shut down, some switching to delivery while others closed their doors completely, unable to make payroll on their newly reduced revenue.

This "novel coronavirus," whatever it was, had my attention.

*

Like many Americans, I was lucky.

Almost all my work could be done via Zoom and conference calls.

My team and I didn't have to worry about losing our jobs or our incomes because of the virus. Lawyers could still take depositions and file briefs. While the courtrooms themselves were closed, making it impossible to hold trials, we could still do status conferences and other administrative meetings. We still argued remotely in appellate cases, but our criminal cases—on which we had been laser-focused during our first year in office—were all put off indefinitely.

I announced that all 350 people in my office should begin working from home immediately. So did every other office of the state government. For guidance, we looked to the White House, where President Trump had been appearing in public with a rotating cast of people from the public health bureaucracy: Dr. Anthony Fauci, the director of the National Institute of Allergy and Infectious Diseases, who became the face of the federal response; Dr. Deborah Birx, the White House coronavirus response coordinator; and Surgeon General Dr. Jerome Adams.

Every time Fauci, Birx, and Adams (especially Fauci) stepped up to the microphone, they assured us that they knew best. They had spent decades in public health. They told us that we needed to trust the Science™ and that anyone who didn't was putting our country at serious risk of mass death. In almost no time at all, we saw the rise of the Experts™, a class of people who, on the Left at least, were treated as unquestionable authorities. Their guidance wasn't just about science—it became a political litmus test. In those early months, no one truly knew the right answers, but that uncertainty quickly turned into a moral divide: the prevailing narrative was less about following science and more about portraying conservatives as heartless villains who cared only about keeping factories open while people died. What started as a pivot from Trump to the all-knowing Dr. Fauci took on a strange, then authoritarian, turn when Trump left office.

I'm sure you remember that in March 2020, when we had barely come up with the name "Covid-19," we needed that evidence-based guidance desperately. Bad information was everywhere. As I walked the streets of Glendale, Missouri, wearing AirPods to take part in senior staff calls figuring out how to run a state AG's office during a pandemic, there were rumors that the virus could live for days on surfaces. I saw videos of people on social media scrubbing their groceries with disinfectant and handling everyday household items with rubber gloves. In the quiet, suburban streets outside my house, people on walks avoided one another, crossing the street when others were within thirty feet. For a few weeks, it felt like we were living through the end of the world.

And as the weeks wore on, I noticed that some people seemed to be enjoying the end of the world a whole lot more than others. Take Dr. Fauci, for instance. From the minute he showed up on the major news shows during those early days of the pandemic, it was difficult not to detect a sense of glee on the little guy's face. He seemed to love the attention. In hindsight, it isn't hard to see how this supposedly objective scientist ended up posing for *In Style* magazine and answering interview questions about his morning routine. The pursuit of power, influence, and public adulation seemed to be his main objective. The same might be said of all the other Covid-19 pundits who showed up in March and April of 2020, some of whom had worked in the Obama Administration, others of whom had anointed themselves Experts™ in virology and epidemiology overnight. (Soon they'd also become Experts™ in election law, Ukrainian history, and the Middle East—especially Afghanistan.)

Perhaps that is why the guidance that these Experts™ gave never seemed to add up. One day, we were told that masks were ineffective. Dr. Fauci himself said on national television that there was "no reason to be walking around with a mask." (We now know that he was privately giving the same advice to his close friends, such as senior officials from the Obama Administration like Sylvia Burwell.)[1] Then, without any new information or peer-reviewed studies, we were told that anyone who didn't wear a mask was putting his or her neighbors in serious danger of contracting Covid-19. Later, of course, we would learn exactly what was happening. Dr. Fauci and others like him changed their public advice about masks based on whether masks were available to health care workers at the time. They were *lying*, in other words.

Regardless of their motives, this was wrong. They abandoned the principle of telling the truth and letting people make their own decisions. Instead they manipulated data and the truth to control people. This is a dangerous game to play. The universe abhors a vacuum, so instead of debate, we had lies.

Although I do look back fondly at the dinners made together as a family, the games of Uno and watching eighties movies with my kids, and being obsessed with Netflix's *The Last Dance* and *Tiger King* in those first few weeks, there was something sci fi–level wrong with what was happening. Reviewing all of this now, I'm reminded of an experiment conducted by the Israeli American economist Dan Ariely, who was once interviewed for a documentary on the disgraced entrepreneur Elizabeth Holmes titled *Out for Blood*. In explaining why Holmes could have lied to so many people for so long, Ariely recounts an experiment he once conducted involving a six-sided die. According to a summary of the experiment published by the Foundation for Economic Education, researchers

> *had participants roll for a monetary reward corresponding to the number on the die. If the die landed on the number 4, the individual was paid $4; if they rolled a 6, they'd receive $6. Before rolling, however, participants were asked to decide which side of the die— bottom or top—determined the dollar amount they'd receive. Participants were told to not tell the researchers their choice, but to mark this on a piece of paper. Essentially, participants could make more money by simply lying—and that's what many did.*

"When people [rolled] 20 times, we found that they were incredibly lucky," said Ariely. "Not lucky 100 percent of the time, but maybe 13 or 14 times."

His experiment did not end there, however. Ariely conducted the same experiment, but with people connected to a lie detector. Did people still cheat? Yes, and the lie detector confirms this. (Not always and not perfectly, Ariely concedes.) But the real twist comes when researchers conducted the same experiment but told participants the money they earn will be donated to a charity of their choice.[2]

What happens?

"People cheat more," Ariely says. "And the lie detector stops working."

To summarize, people can do horrible things when they think they're acting for the "greater good." When Dr. Fauci lied to the American people about masks, and later a great many other things, he set in motion a level of groupthink and Covid authoritarianism that unleashed new levels of Othering in the U.S.—and, whatever he thought he was doing at the time, the results were definitive and devastating for so many lives and livelihoods.

As the weeks wore on, these supposedly noble lies piled up. We were told that it would only take fifteen days to "slow the spread" of the virus and "flatten the curve" of infection. I have no doubt that Dr. Fauci and Dr. Deborah Birx, both of whom were ubiquitous at the podium by that time, knew that we were in for a *much* longer lockdown. A conditioning was happening. The power they amassed may have even been surprising to them, but clearly it was intoxicating. With what we all saw in China, they must have known they were lying to President Trump and the American people. Even if you assume the best intentions, the fact was that anyone who stood against them would simply be tarred as antiscience or anti-intellectual. As we explore in later chapters, this effort became serial.

Suddenly the Experts™ were everywhere. Anyone who'd ever taken a biology course in high school came to believe that he or she had the right to wield the Science™ like a cudgel against those who didn't believe we should stay locked down forever. It didn't take long for the heads of our nation's major social media companies—the employees of which leaned *way* to the left at the time—to get in on the action. Dr. Scott Atlas, a Trump Administration advisor, was locked out of his Twitter account after listing places where Covid-19 cases had surged despite mask mandates. He later deleted his account. Major universities were willing to fire faculty who questioned the Science™.

Meanwhile, conditions on the ground grew worse by the day. In Michigan, where Governor Gretchen Whitmer imposed some of the strictest lockdowns in the nation—including bans on traveling and purchasing certain goods—it became increasingly difficult for residents to live their lives. In California, Governor Gavin Newsom restricted outdoor dining and private gatherings while deciding for himself that it was safe to dine indoors, maskless, with friends at an exclusive Napa Valley restaurant called The French Laundry. These politicians believed they were capable of determining when they and their allies were safe but did not allow normal Americans to make those same decisions for themselves—despite the fact that cases consistently rose and fell in every country, regardless of policy, as individuals adjusted their own behavior. As the world watched the daily press conferences of New York Governor Andrew Cuomo with an increasing mix of confusion and alarm, more than 15,000 people perished of Covid-19 in the state's nursing homes, largely thanks to a directive from the governor that forced Covid-positive patients into facilities with vulnerable elderly people. Worship services were canceled. Businesses failed. People were forced to watch their family members die on FaceTime due to the restrictions placed on hospital visiting hours.

Today we can only estimate the devastation caused by these lockdowns. A study conducted by the Well Being Trust and the Robert Graham Center revealed that "deaths of despair" (meaning suicides, overdoses, and other such avoidable deaths) increased by about 10 percent during the pandemic, a number that suggests up to 75,000 additional deaths. This was especially prevalent among young people, many of whom were ripped away from their peers in school at the worst time in their development. Looking back, we can see that such deaths were inevitable—and foreseeable. When a society takes away church, community, and all sense of meaning in the name of the Science™, it shouldn't be surprising that bad things happen.

To the pundit class and the public health Experts™ who made the decisions, these consequences were negligible. It makes sense. With almost no exceptions, reporters and government workers could spend the early days of the pandemic working from home on their laptops. Most of their work could be done over Zoom, just like my own. When they got hungry, they ordered food from DoorDash or Grubhub, never giving a second thought to the "essential worker" who still had to put on a mask, pick up their food, and drive it all the way out to their homes.

These people were happy to prolong the lockdown. In some sense, it was good for them—just as it was good for online shipping giants like Amazon to crush small, locally owned companies that compete for their business. For years they had been warning that President Donald Trump was a chaotic force in our politics who would soon drag the country down into despair and chaos. All that time, nothing but great things had happened. Now that they finally had a good crisis to pin on the guy—one that was clearly inevitable, given the communicability of the disease and the failure of the Chinese Communist Party to deal with it swiftly enough at the outset—they weren't going to let it go. Instead they were going to follow the play-book and milk the crisis for all it was worth. As Rahm Emanuel, the former chief of staff to President Barack Obama and mayor of Chicago, once said, "Never let a good crisis go to waste."

For those who study history—and communism specifically—demoralization is critical to fundamentally changing a society. You have to untether people from the things that hold them together: their faith, their sense of community, their belief in their country. The Left couldn't believe their good fortune. Maybe it didn't start that way, but they quickly understood the power they could galvanize. In the months and years to come, the liberal establishment would capitalize on the crisis of Covid-19 in unprecedented ways, dragging the United States into a new era. They told us the virus should fundamentally change the way we conducted elections and that we needed to make the untested mRNA "vaccines" mandatory. They told American citizens they couldn't travel because of the virus, while allowing millions of illegal migrants to enter without testing.

But their motivations weren't just about power—they also thought this was their "FAFO" moment. They believed Covid would purge conservatives and force everyone else into the arms of the Left, finally allowing them to say, *I told you so.* They were certain that the most progressive, state-controlled countries would come out ahead, while defenders of freedom would be wiped out. Every new rule, every shifting mandate, was a way to reinforce this belief. The hypocrisy was too much for most people to bear, and slowly, many began to feel powerless against a system that was rewriting the rules by the day.

Different people would have different breaking points—moments when they would look around at the ridiculous rules of the new regime and say, "Enough." For some people, it would be the moment they first read the letter, signed by more than one thousand public health officials, that gave people permission to go outside and gather in large groups, just as long as those large groups were protesting "systemic racism" rather than lockdowns. This letter, which came out in the summer of 2020 as our cities were being looted and burned by violent left-wing mobs, read:

> On April 30, heavily armed and predominantly white protestors entered the State Capitol Building in Lansing, Michigan, protesting stay-at-home orders and calls for widespread public masking to prevent the spread of COVID-19. Infectious disease physicians and public health officials publicly condemned these actions and privately mourned the widening rift between leaders in science and a subset of the communities that they serve. As of May 30, we are witnessing continuing demonstrations in response to ongoing, pervasive, and lethal institutional racism set off by the killings of George Floyd and Breonna Taylor, among many other Black lives taken by police. A public health response to these demonstrations is also warranted, but this message must be wholly different from the response to white protesters resisting stay-home orders. Infectious disease and public health narratives adjacent to demonstrations against racism must be consciously anti-racist, and infectious disease experts must be clear and consistent in prioritizing an anti-racist message. **White supremacy is a lethal public health issue that predates and contributes to COVID-19. . . . Protests against systemic racism, which fosters the disproportionate burden of COVID-19 on Black communities and also perpetuates police violence, must be supported.**[3]

Even now, after all we've learned about the tendency of public health officials to "make it up as they go" (to use the technical term), it's hard to believe that they could have released such a ridiculous letter with straight faces. It's one of the many things that I'm sure Dr. Fauci, Kamala Harris, and the rest of the Experts™ would like you to forget. I can see why even the people who'd been the most trusting of the Science™ finally threw up their hands and decided that they'd had enough of biased public health bureaucrats telling them what to do.

Reading that letter today, most of us can see that these people were blatantly lying. They wanted to get out of the house and protest, and so they twisted the Science™ to fit their preferences. When it was Republicans who wanted to speak out against lockdowns—which, as stated earlier, were responsible for death and devastation on a massive scale—everyone had to stay inside and do what they were told. When those on the Left wanted to hit the streets, the Science™ magically changed. In a way, this is a stark reminder of just how important our legal system is. I couldn't imagine how any of these scientists would have defended the proposition "Covid is dangerous, unless you're protesting racism" in court.

Of course, my breaking point came earlier.

Much earlier.

*

It was March 2020, and I had just finished a phone call with a man who owned a chain of grocery stores in Missouri. He had let me know that because of supply-chain issues, he was worried about "runs" on his stores.

For a moment, I was stunned. I, like most people in the United States, had believed for years that this kind of thing simply couldn't happen in our country. Runs on banks and grocery stores were the kinds of things that tended to happen in third-world, postsocialist banana republics, not the most successful and prosperous republic in world history. But as I considered the evidence that my friend the grocery store owner was presenting to me, I began wondering how close we really were to total chaos. If you took social interaction and the ability to purchase food and basic goods away from people, how many days of peace and stability did we really have left? Was it three days? A week? Our global supply chain networks were more fragile than people assumed. The more I looked into it, the more I discovered the crossroads of the global supply chains were in the People's Republic of China. Critical minerals, materials of every kind, and even materials we need for all manners of pharmaceuticals—all sourced from China. I began to realize the anti-epileptic drugs my son relied on every day to stay alive could be cut off. This is true for millions upon billions of people worldwide in various ways. China also happened to be the place where the virus originated, and their increasing aggressive demeanor on the world stage demanded that the role they played in this pandemic be examined. But how in the world could I do that?

That realization and question lay in the backdrop of what was happening on the ground and in Washington, where President Trump and members of Congress worked on measures like the Paycheck Protection Program (PPP). Democrats were also seizing on a new narrative to use against President Trump, who had kept enough of his campaign promises to earn himself a second term, all while he was working hard on the rest. In fact, Democrats seemed hell-bent on exploiting the crisis. Every time bad news came in, they got to pin it on Trump, which they believed would help them in the upcoming 2020 election. When the President spoke out against lockdowns, saying that "the cure cannot be worse than the disease," they said he was failing to "follow the science." They rarely mentioned that the science was hardly mature and lockdowns had never been advisable before. As we've seen recently, many of the numbers that were thrown at us during those early days—the ten-day quarantine rule, the six-feet-apart mandate—were based on nothing but guesswork, which would have been more acceptable if that guesswork hadn't been presented to us as hard and fast science from the Experts™.

As this was all playing out in March and April 2020, my office was active in protecting Missourians and handling the day-to-day job as AG, but I felt we could do more. So did the members of my team. All over Missouri, people were suffering. They were angry. Every day, I heard from people who wanted answers about why *this* virus— which started out just like so many of the other pandemics that never happened—had ushered in a global crisis. People wanted to know who was responsible for ushering the Covid-19 pandemic into the world, elevating what might have been a minor localized epidemic into a global catastrophe. Even in those early days, all signs pointed to the Chinese Communist Party. Right away, we knew that the disease had come from the Chinese city of Wuhan, a major transportation hub that just so happened to have a giant building called the WUHAN INSTITUTE OF VIROLOGY right in the center.

Throughout March, as the disease spread and the death count mounted, I began reading reports of exactly what had occurred at the highest levels of the Chinese government during the first hours of the Covid-19 pandemic. I read a shocking account of a Chinese doctor, Li Wenliang, who had attempted to warn a group of friends about the new virus using WeChat. He had also reposted a note from another doctor who'd treated patients suffering from an unknown disease. For this, according to an account published later by the journalist Lawrence Wright, he was charged by the Chinese Communist Party (CCP) with "rumor mongering that 'severely disturbed the social order.'" He was forced to sign a confession. His punishment, and that of seven other doctors who had publicly discussed the outbreak, was broadcast on China Central Television, a clear message to others who might attempt to undermine the Communist government's narrative."[4]

That narrative, for the time being, was that the virus we'd soon come to call Covid-19 could not be spread from person to person. Even in late December, the Chinese government had attempted to bolster this narrative by censoring phrases such as "Wuhan wet market" or "Wuhan disease" using its internet firewall. An interview with the doctor who originally posted a note about the transmissibility of Covid-19 was taken down from the internet. On February 6, long after Covid-19 had spread from Wuhan—a key transportation hub in China, which, according to *The New York Times*, saw 175,000 people leave the city on January 1 alone—Dr. Li died. According to Wright, "He left behind a five-year-old child and a pregnant wife. The mass mourning that greeted his death was an expression of the anguish expressed by great numbers of Chinese people. They saw Li as a whistleblower and a martyr for free speech. They laid flowers in front of the Wuhan hospital and blew whistles in his honor all over China. It was a telling indicator of the provisional nature of CCP rule. Before he died, Dr. Li told *Caixin* magazine, 'A healthy society shouldn't have only one voice.'"[5]

Unfortunately, the "one voice" with which the CCP spoke was strong, and many organizations—primarily the World Health Organization, whose leader never missed an opportunity to side with China—were willing to listen. Officials at the CCP stalled, obfuscated, and lied until it was far too late to contain the virus to Wuhan.

Later, of course, we would learn that these were the very government officials with whom Dr. Fauci and other Experts™ in the United States had been working to conduct "gain of function" research on novel coronaviruses. Fauci has repeatedly denied his funding of labs creating novel coronaviruses with enhanced infectivity is funding gain of function research. Thanks to a deposition of Dr. Fauci that my office would take in a case called *Missouri v. Biden*, we know that he sent his deputy to China not long after all this occurred, and that the deputy convinced Dr. Fauci that the United States should emulate China's "extreme" lockdown measures. We also know that, during this same time, Dr. Fauci was scrambling behind the scenes to discredit and censor the eminently plausible theory that Covid-19 escaped from the Wuhan Institute of Virology. (But that's a story for another chapter.)

During those confusing early weeks, all we knew was that China had done just about every bad thing that was possible to do in the first hours of a pandemic. They had lied about the severity of the disease and made it illegal for anyone to contradict them. Even then, we had reports of doctors who'd been jailed and socially ostracized for trying to get the word out about the novel (previously unidentified) coronavirus. We knew that the Chinese government could have acted and didn't. There were also troubling reports that the masks and personal protective equipment that the party was sending to other countries as a show of solidarity were faulty. Several countries had reported receiving faulty masks. Most of the personal protective equipment (PPE) didn't even work. On the flip side, there were credible and disturbing reports that, during the first days of the pandemic—when Chinese Communist officials knew that the virus had escaped and was highly contagious, but suppressed this information from reaching the world—China began buying up and hoarding the high-quality PPE needed to treat Covid patients from other countries.

The picture was slowly coming into focus. But I had seen enough to know that we needed to take action. As I read about the horrific actions that the CCP had taken—or, more importantly, *failed* to take during these early days—a question nagged at me.

If this is what I can find out just by reading the newspaper, I wondered, *what have they managed to keep hidden?*

I decided to find out.

One morning in early April, I sat down with John Sauer, who'd served as my solicitor general in Missouri. John now serves as the solicitor general of the United States. (I was proud to advocate for him for that role with President Trump and honored to introduce him at his hearing in front of the Senate Judiciary Committee.) In addition to being an easy guy to work with, John also happens to be a certified legal genius. He thinks outside the box like no one I've ever met. As we were discussing the origins of the virus and potential legal remedies for the people of Missouri, we walked through a crazy idea—which, as we talked through potential ways to make it happen, didn't seem so crazy after all. It was only a few minutes later that we had come up with a plan.

Soon Missouri was going to become the first U.S. state ever to sue the Chinese Communist Party.

And we were going to win.

Chapter 2

SCHMITT V. THE PEOPLE'S
REPUBLIC OF CHINA

Can we even *do* that?"

It was early April 2020, after the scrubbing-all-the-groceries phase of Covid, but a little before the everyone-is-baking-sourdough-bread phase. For the past few minutes, I had been telling a few members of my team about my plan to file a lawsuit against China—as in, the *country* of China—for unleashing the novel coronavirus on the world. As I walked along the Glendale streets near my home, racking up about 25,000 steps a day while on the phone, I dodged the background sounds that punctuated every call: the rumble of the trash truck outside, car doors slamming, the occasional neighbor yelling at their dog to come inside. These sounds, muffling the voices on the other end, meant I couldn't catch their immediate reactions. But I had a feeling that at least a few of them were wondering if I was serious or pulling a belated April Fools prank.

Justin Smith chimed in. Back in March, I had promoted Justin from the head of our special litigation unit—kind of like a legal SEAL team, willing to take on special projects with their particular set of skills—to the person overseeing all 350 lawyers in the office. It was a big job, and he'd gotten it at a challenging time. But he had also been instrumental in my early efforts to understand every aspect of the China case we were about to file.

"We think so," he said.

I understood some of the staff's hesitation. They were lawyers, after all. At some point during their legal education, they had learned about the doctrine of foreign sovereign immunity, which protects foreign countries from being sued in U.S. courts in many circumstances. According to the Foreign Sovereign Immunities Act of 1976 (FSIA), offices like mine typically could not drag representatives of China into a courthouse in Cape Girardeau, Missouri, and force them to answer for their clear violations of the law. But that doctrine is not absolute.

I should say that in a vast majority of cases, this law serves a very important purpose. It prevents the U.S. court system from getting bogged down in frivolous, politically motivated lawsuits, for one thing. I can only imagine what our legal system would look like if private citizens were allowed to sue foreign countries at will. We might end up with lines of people wanting to file complaints against Italy because their long-planned vacations didn't go well; we might have people trying to take India to court for their high levels of carbon emissions. Nothing would ever get done again.

More than anything, the FSIA encourages diplomatic solutions to problems. When two countries have issues with one another, it's important that they know the only option is sitting down at a table and talking it out. If the option to sue were in play, there isn't a country in the world that wouldn't go that route instead. Sovereign immunity is also important because of reciprocity. The United States tacitly agrees not to file suit against other countries in American courts, and as such, we expect not to be dragged into courts overseas every time there's a problem. The FSIA law thus discourages retaliation against the United States and U.S. citizens by foreign nations in foreign courts where the rule of law is less well preserved than here.

However, as the team and I dug deeper into the actions of the Chinese Communist Party during the early days of the pandemic, we became convinced that we were dealing with one of the rare cases in which foreign sovereign immunity should not apply. Within the text of the FSIA law itself, there are exceptions that allow foreign countries to be sued. If, for instance, a country engages in an act of state-sponsored terrorism that affects American citizens, those citizens have the right to sue the country in American courts. Recently, we've seen it happen in a case involving a group of Americans who successfully filed suit against the nation of Saudi Arabia, alleging that that country helped finance the terror attacks of September 11, 2001.

To prosecute the Chinese Communist Party, my team relied on FSIA's commercial-activity exception. This allows for legal action against foreign states if the lawsuit is based on a foreign state's commercial activity that has a direct effect in the United States.

The full text of the commercial activity exception states:

A foreign state shall not be immune from the jurisdiction of courts of the United States or of the States in any case . . . in which the action is based upon a commercial activity carried on in the United States by the foreign state; or upon an act performed in the United States in connection with a commercial activity of the foreign state elsewhere; or upon an act outside the territory of the United States in connection with a commercial activity of the foreign state elsewhere and that act causes a direct effect in the United States.

This seemed to describe the actions of the People's Republic of China and the Chinese Communist Party perfectly. Also, there was an important question whether the Communist *Party* (as opposed to the communist government) is a foreign sovereign at all. The party itself publicly insists that it is *not* the government, but that it is separate and distinct from the government, just one political party among many—implying that the doctrine of foreign sovereign immunity does not apply to it. The same argument applied to some other entities we sued, including the Wuhan Institute of Virology.

Although there was certainly a case to be made, especially in those early days, that the actions of the CCP constituted terrorism (especially considering the lies they had spread about the virus), we believed that the commercial-activity exception was the most viable option for litigation. At the very least, it was the thing that was least likely to be thrown out of court by an unfriendly judge.

The logic was simple. During those crucial early weeks of the virus, when the evidence was mounting that Covid-19 was going to become a deadly, highly communicable disease, the CCP had knowledge about the virus that no one else in the world had. They knew that it could be transmitted via the air. They knew that it was likely to spread, and they believed that preventing its transmission would require an enormous number of masks, gloves, and other PPE. That, it seemed, was why they hoarded that equipment, the vast majority of which was manufactured in China and sold to the world through companies that were effectively shell corporations controlled by the CCP. Thus there were multiple reports that China was buying up and hoarding large quantities of high-quality PPE from Western countries through intermediaries—usually Chinese companies and Chinese nationals living abroad—while it was exporting low-quality PPE to the same countries.

That, it seemed, was behavior that we could hold the CCP and others accountable for. It was simple, it was obviously "commercial," and someone without a law degree could understand it. China controlled the world's supply of personal protective equipment. Then China unleashed a deadly pandemic on the world, told no one, canceled flights within the country from Wuhan but not to the rest of the world, and began purchasing and hoarding the best PPE for itself while (allegedly) shipping all the defective stuff out to other countries, the United States of America included.

For me, that was personal. My son, Stephen, was born with a rare genetic condition. Every day, he takes medications in liquid form through his G-tube, all of which were manufactured to some degree in China. And if the CCP had, in some way, been willing to send out defective PPE to other countries, there was no guarantee that they wouldn't start doing it with medications in the future. Luckily, we hadn't yet encountered this problem. But the first months of Covid-19 saw shortages of all kinds of medications.

PPE was one thing. But if China didn't suffer consequences for its actions this time around, there was no telling what would happen during the next pandemic—not to mention if this sort of thing were ever weaponized. Defective medications might be shipped out. *Poison* medications might be shipped out. *No* medications might be shipped out. If I had learned anything watching China in recent years, it was that you should never underestimate the Communist Party's capacity for depravity and retribution. In part I hoped that our lawsuit, even if it didn't succeed in bringing in the billions of dollars we estimated the pandemic cost Missourians, would reveal some of that depravity to the public. Sometimes the discovery phase of litigation—during which key players in malfeasance can be deposed and documents must be handed over—can be as important, and illuminating, as any verdict.

Over the next few days, my team and I conducted thorough research and began laying out our case. This was a process that typically took a few months, but we wanted to move quickly. Given that everything in the country was still shut down at the time, it wasn't like any of us had anywhere to be. I read everything I could get my hands on about the conduct of the Chinese government during the early hours of the pandemic; so did Justin and John and the solicitor team, who were smart and thorough. By the middle of April we were ready to draft the federal complaint against the People's Republic of China, the Chinese Communist Party, and other entities in China, including the Wuhan Institution of Virology, when many others wouldn't even utter the name for fear of being called a conspiracy theorist or a racist. John and his team in the solicitor general's office did a phenomenal job with it.

On one level, a complaint or petition is simply the first step in a lawsuit. It tells the person or company—or, in our case, the *country*—what they're being accused of, and it lays out in precise detail how they have violated the law, and then it asks for a remedy or damages. The complaint needs to be formatted according to some pretty technical guidelines, and there are key elements that need to be included. A judge will toss it out, for instance, if it doesn't state a claim upon which relief can be granted. Basically, you have to allege facts that if proven to be true actually make the other side liable or guilty in a criminal case. These finely wrought procedures are important because our system is based on rules and precedent. That is, judges make decisions based on prior decisions by other judges, some dating back to the years immediately following the founding of our country, and in some instances further back than that, as our system was built on English common law that traveled across the Atlantic along with the *Mayflower*.

One often-overlooked aspect of the complaint or petition is that it needs to tell a compelling story, especially when it's going to be as widely read as ours. The story needs to include all the elements you might expect from a novel: characters, motivations, and clear stakes. And the story must be told in language that is clear, concise, and easy for the average person to digest. Anyone with a fifth-grade reading level who would read it should be able to flip through it in a few minutes and get the gist of who's being pursued and why. Again, this is a reminder of why courts are so important. When you have a story that makes sense—which conservatives usually do—a courtroom gives you a perfect venue to tell that story.

So, John and the team got to work compiling all the research we'd done, working in record time to produce a complaint that was thorough and lucid. To support our claims, we included all the details of what had happened in the complaint. It was important for the American people to understand everything that China had done to put us all in such danger.

On the first page of the complaint, we laid out the origins of the pandemic as clearly as possible, citing all known reports of what had happened in Wuhan, China, during those crucial days in December 2019 and January 2021.

The first page read:

In this case, the State of Missouri seeks recovery for the enormous loss of life, human suffering, and economic turmoil experienced by all Missourians for the COVID-19 pandemic that has disrupted the entire world. An appalling campaign of deceit, concealment, misfeasance, and inaction by Chinese authorities unleashed the pandemic. During the critical weeks of the initial outbreak, Chinese authorities deceived the public, suppressed crucial information, arrested whistleblowers, denied human-to-human transmission in the face of mounting evidence, destroyed critical medical research, permitted millions of people to be exposed to the virus, and even hoarded personal protective equipment—thus causing a global pandemic that was unnecessary and preventable. Defendants are responsible for the enormous death, suffering, and economic losses they inflicted on the world, including Missourians, and they should be held accountable.

Then we laid out the exact timeline of events as we knew it at the time, including every step that the CCP took to conceal the truth of what was happening from the world. We identified the parties—including the sentence "defendant is a Communist Nation in Asia"—and listed the allegations. Later, our timeline would become the basis for a lot of people and pundits who wanted to examine the malfeasance of the CCP in other lawsuits, as well as academic papers and books. It was the first time anyone had bothered to compile evidence from many sources and paint a clear picture of wrongdoing.

It was perfect.

But the next steps would be challenging and complicated.

*

If you want to sue someone in the American legal system, you have to serve them first.

In short, this means that you need to notify the person you're suing that they have, in fact, been sued, you have to provide them with the legal papers you have filed, and you have to have a clear record of when that person was notified. Anyone who has ever had a guy in a fake delivery outfit show up to your door with papers pertaining to a lawsuit will know exactly what I'm talking about.

In most cases, the men and women who show up at people's doorsteps work for "process servers." These folks have decided they like delivering bad news to other people and made a career out of it. When the process server delivers papers, they will report to the court that the papers were delivered at a certain time, in a certain location, and to a certain person. That starts the lawsuit shot clock.

This, as you might imagine, was a little difficult when it came to our China suit. I couldn't just call up a local sheriff and put him on a plane to Beijing with a copy of our complaint in his hand and tell him to deliver it straight to the offices of President Xi Jinping. So we dug into the rules. As it turned out, the first step was notifying China of our intent to sue in accordance with a few specific provisions of the Hague Convention. Ratified at the turn of the twentieth century, the Hague Convention is a series of treaties that set up long-standing rules governing what nations can and cannot do to one another on the world stage. According to these provisions, when one country—or one *state* in a country, in our case—wants to sue another, they must notify the other via diplomatic means. Then the other country has the ability to challenge the suit and say it's baseless.

However, the Chinese Communist Party never officially responded to us. We expected them to, but it never happened. Luckily, we had other ways of getting the lawsuit through. The federal rules allowed us to ask the court to authorize alternative methods of service, including service by email—which the court did authorize. Thus, one of the first steps (as crazy as this might sound) was tracking down email addresses for the CCP and other defendants. We had already arranged for a company in Tennessee to translate our complaint into Chinese and sent over a PDF version, just like you'd do with a document in any normal office job. But this wasn't some TPS report. To the CCP, where they manage their world reputation with carrots and big sticks, this would be no small deal. And because we had to file a motion in court to authorize service by email, they knew the emails were coming. I'm sure it won't surprise you to learn that several email accounts were set to reject our email when the complaint went out. Luckily we had identified alternative email addresses for many defendants, so some of the emails went through on a second or third attempt.

For the other defendants, there was one final option in the federal rules, which involves coordination with the U.S. State Department. In extreme circumstances, special deliveries of documents could be made via "diplomatic pouch," which, amazingly, is exactly what it sounds like—a small pouch made of paper that goes over to China on a plane and gets hand-delivered by a rep from our State Department to Chinese officials. This pouch left the United States on April 12, and we got word that the Chinese government had received it on April 15.

It was on.

*

As we put the case together, we prepared for retribution from China. I told my team to be careful with all their electronic communications, which might very well be under Chinese surveillance. After all, China's foreign minister had made a public statement criticizing our lawsuit the day it was filed. In Washington, it is not uncommon for elected officials and their aides to leave phones in drawers out of fear that the Chinese government might be listening in—which, as I've learned in the years since, they usually are.

What we *didn't* expect, of course, was the resistance we'd get from people here in the United States, especially Democrats, for being too tough on China. Today it's hard to imagine how strange the attitude of the Left was during those first days of Covid-19. Rather than directing their anger and frustration about the coronavirus toward China, they aimed it straight at President Trump, who was clearly doing the best that he could to lead the United States through an unprecedented, once-in-a-century crisis. In January and February, as the virus was spreading, it was virtually forbidden on the Left to say anything negative about China. Anyone who even came close was labeled a racist.

In late January, for instance, President Trump took the unprecedented step of shutting down travel from China, making only rare exceptions for people holding U.S. passports. The very next day, Joe Biden tweeted, We are in the midst of a crisis with the coronavirus. We need to lead the way with science—not Donald Trump's record of hysteria, xenophobia, and fear-mongering. He is the worst possible person to lead our country through a global health emergency. That same day, he said, "This is no time for Donald Trump's record of hysteria, xenophobia—hysterical xenophobia—to . . . fear mongering, to lead the way instead of science." Days earlier, Biden's future chief of staff Ron Klain—who, presumably, was crafting most of Biden's messaging at the time—said that a travel ban in late January would have been "premature."

If anything, the opposite was the case. As the historian Niall Ferguson writes in his book *Doom: The Politics of Catastrophe*, "The virus spread at the speed of a jet plane" in January 2020, moving "through the scale-free network of international passenger airports, expedited by the unprecedented volume of journeys in December 2019 and January 2020, more than double the level of fifteen years before."

A few weeks later, Speaker of the House Nancy Pelosi stood on the streets of San Francisco, encouraging people to gather in crowds to celebrate Chinese New Year. Speaking to reporters in February 2020, she said, "What we're trying to do today is say everything is fine here.... Come because precautions have been taken. The city is on top of the situation.... All I can say is, 'I'm here.' We feel safe and sound, so many of us coming here."

This wasn't some fringe view at the time. During the early days of the pandemic, anyone who dared suggest that China bore some responsibility for the virus—or who pointed out, correctly, that unrestricted travel was a primary means of its spread—was vilified by Democrats. Hakeem Jeffries, then the head of the House Democratic Caucus, tweeted that Trump was the Xenophobe. In. Chief. Tim Kaine, Hillary Clinton's old running mate, tweeted that the travel ban was a Pathetic attempt to shift blame from his Visible Incompetence to an Invisible Enemy. The president needs to re-read the Declaration of Independence, criticizing King George for restricting immigration to America.

In late April 2020, just after Tim Kaine sent that tweet, we learned that our complaint against the People's Republic of China had been filed, and that the lawsuit could move forward. The first shot in a long, drawn-out legal war had been fired.

And China, as expected, was not happy about it.

*

Almost immediately, Chinese state-run media began running threats from high-ranking officials about the retaliatory steps that would be taken against me and several other American politicians who had taken up the fight against China. A report published in the state-run newspaper *Global Times* suggested that China would renegotiate trade deals specifically to hurt the state of Missouri. A representative of the CCP said, "We must resolutely hit back at those politicians who, for no reason, undermine China-U.S. ties for their own political benefits. For those who promote anti-China legislation, we need to find out what the business ties are between those officials or their families with China. We can't just strike back symbolically, but we should impose countermeasures that could make them feel the pain."[1]

I remember cracking open a few Busch Lights in a parking lot near my house with my friend Jim Monafo in those early Covid days, when bars and restaurants were closed, and admitting to him that seeing a representative of the Chinese Communist Party—which has made plenty of people "feel the pain" over the years—take direct aim at me wasn't on my bingo card and was a little uncomfortable at first, but I settled into the chair of protagonist in this important story. And unlike some Democrats in the United States (specifically Joe Biden, Nancy Pelosi, and Hillary Clinton), my family didn't have any business interests in China. Also, I had learned during my research that you couldn't exactly take the Chinese *Global Times* at its word. It was propaganda. This was the paper, after all, that had spread dangerous misinformation about the coronavirus during those crucial early hours, covering up for the failures of the Chinese Communist Party at the highest levels. The paper had lied about the virus to calm the masses (sound familiar?) by stating the virus couldn't spread from person to person, and it was probably engaged in an intimidation game regarding the serious retaliatory measures against me. In the end, I was banned from China, which I consider a badge of honor. So far, no other harm has befallen me.

Our case, on the other hand, got viciously attacked in the press for the same reasons that Democrats didn't like it. It shifted blame away from Trump and to the country that unleashed the virus on the world. There was a legal bump in the road in 2022, when the judge dismissed the claims, stating that Missouri could not sue the Chinese Communist Party. However, in early 2024, the U.S. Court of Appeals for the Eighth Circuit reversed that decision, ruling that the commercial-activity exception portion of the case could stand.

On March 7, 2025, a federal judge ruled that China was responsible for misleading the world about Covid-19 and for hoarding personal protective equipment, worsening the crisis for Americans. The court awarded Missouri over $24 billion in damages—the largest judgment in state history. That means one thing: Missouri can now seize Chinese-owned assets, including farmland, to make them pay. We had led the way. Missouri took on the CCP and won. Other states and private citizens looking to hold China accountable now have a road map. My successor, Andrew Bailey, has been relentless in carrying this fight across the finish line, and I couldn't be prouder of him. Now he can go seize assets of China.

Missouri isn't just the Show Me State—we're the Show Me the Money State now.

Of course, this was only the first of many cases my team and I filed in response to the Covid-19 pandemic. Although the rest were confined to the United States, they were just as contentious as the China lawsuit. And like the China suit, they got to the very heart of what it means to live in a free country.

Chapter 3

THE LEFT'S DARK MONEY
V. THE VOTERS

When you serve as Attorney General, you get to play offense, but you also spend a lot of time playing defense—defending lawsuits, defending laws passed by the legislature, defending the Constitution, defending individual liberty, and more. As someone who grew up playing sports, including football and baseball in college, playing defense wasn't a foreign concept to me; in fact, it was second nature. Looking back, I realized that in almost every sport, I had played positions where I was the last line of defense. In baseball, I was out in the outfield; in basketball, I played in the paint; in grade school soccer, I played sweeper; and in football, I was the free safety. I suppose I always embraced that role and the responsibility it carried.

More than that, I'd never had much tolerance for bullies and wasn't afraid to stand up to them, even from a young age. I remember, specifically, in seventh grade, some guys were picking on a kid with disabilities. Though I was outnumbered, something inside me stirred, and I felt the need to stick up for him, even if it meant a fight, which I wasn't afraid of either. Growing up where I grew up, there was still an honor culture, a code. You needed to stand up for yourself and sometimes that might get physical. In the end, I managed to shame them with words, and the confrontation didn't go further. When I got home and told my dad, he said, "Never let anyone pick on someone who, through no fault of their own, is vulnerable in that way." That advice stuck with me, shaping how I saw the world and my place in it. Later, my son Stephen found his way into our family, reinforcing my commitment to that cause on a much deeper level. I like to think it's part of why God trusted us with him. I suppose I've always fielded the role of defender or protector. So, whether by nature or nurture, the Attorney General role suited me well— especially at that time.

As Attorney General, you face lawsuits against your clients nearly every day. Fortunately, I had a talented team of lawyers whose job was to mount a strong defense. One morning in 2020, during a call with our senior leadership team, I learned that Marc Elias's firm had filed a lawsuit against the state of Missouri, making familiar claims about voter suppression—claims we had already seen in two similar suits filed by the ACLU. These lawsuits challenged Missouri's election integrity laws, specifically targeting the state's notarization requirement for mail-in ballots and voter ID laws. The plaintiffs argued that these measures disproportionately affected minority communities and placed an unconstitutional burden on the right to vote.

The *NAACP v. Missouri* lawsuit focused heavily on Missouri's requirement that voters using mail-in ballots must have their ballot envelopes notarized. The plaintiffs claimed that this requirement was an unfair obstacle, particularly during the Covid-19 pandemic, when finding a notary in person could be more difficult. But the facts told a different story. Missouri law already included exemptions for voters considered "at risk" due to health concerns, and the state had made accommodations to expand access to notary services, including a publicized list of thousands of notaries willing to notarize ballots for free. Additionally, Missouri election law was designed to prioritize in-person voting, with absentee and mail-in ballots serving as a privilege granted under specific conditions, not an unrestricted right.

At its core, these lawsuits were not about stopping voter suppression—they were about weakening safeguards that protect election integrity. The ACLU's lawsuit went even further, attempting to challenge Missouri's voter ID law, arguing that requiring an ID to vote in person was an undue burden, despite the fact that the state provided free identification to anyone who needed it. Their arguments ignored Supreme Court precedent upholding similar laws and overlooked the reality that most industrialized democracies around the world enforce voter ID requirements as a standard election security measure.

I had to roll my eyes. For years, Elias had been a fixture of the Washington, D.C., legal scene. He'd spent most of his career with the law firm Perkins Coie, most famous for working with Hillary Clinton's campaign in 2016. As anyone who's followed the story of the Russia Hoax will know, it was Perkins Coie, specifically Marc Elias, that provided the initial funding to an opposition research firm known as Fusion GPS for what became the Steele Dossier, a packet of salacious (and false) information about Donald Trump collected by a British spy named Christopher Steele. When it turned out that not a single word of that dossier was true—that, in fact, it was a mudslide of unvetted and salacious speculation mostly scooped up by Igor Danchenko, who'd once been investigated for being a Russian agent by the FBI—Elias didn't apologize.

In fact, he pretended he was never involved in the first place.

In October 2017, a reporter at *The Washington Post* named Kenneth P. Vogel wrote a story about the origins of the Steele Dossier that included an account of how Elias funded it. As soon as it came out, Vogel reported on Twitter that Elias "pushed back vigorously, saying, 'You (or your sources) are wrong.'"[1]

All the while, Elias refashioned himself as a supposedly nonpartisan lawyer who stood up for the rights of voters everywhere. This was nonsense, as anyone who studied his record could see. All

Marc Elias and his new firm cared about was making sure Joe Biden and the Democrats prevailed in 2020. If pretending to care about the "rights of disenfranchised voters" was the best way to make that happen, that's what they would do. Even his friends saw through the charade. Speaking to *The New Yorker* in the lead-up to the 2020 election, a law professor at the University of California, Irvine, said, "[Elias] portrays himself as a pro-voter lawyer, but when there is a potential deviation between, say, what voters generically might want, and what Democrats may want, he's going to favor Democrats."[2]

So, to recap: In advance of the most historic election of our lifetimes—one that was taking place against the backdrop of lockdowns pushed largely by Democratic politicians—a left-wing operative who had once used Russian disinformation to try to stop Donald Trump from becoming president in the first place was filing a lawsuit against *my* state to alter Missouri election law to ensure the election of 2020 was conducted fairly and without any interference.

If the stakes weren't so high, I would have laughed.

But the stakes *were* high. For months now, we had seen some of the dirty tricks that the Left was willing to play to secure victory in November 2020. Every day brought a new change to the election procedures, and those changes all seemed to favor Democrats. In almost every case, the Left was claiming that Covid-19 had made it necessary for us to run the 2020 election in a way we'd never run an election before. Elias and his crew claimed that Missouri, like other states, needed to extend the deadline for accepting mail-in ballots; that we needed to drastically lower the standards for voting; and that things like signature matching (which had been used to determine the validity of ballots for years) were no longer necessary.

In reviewing these lawsuits, I could see that they would be easy to beat back, especially with the great team I had assembled in the AG's office. But I wondered why they had come so quickly, and why it seemed that the organizations behind them were so well funded.

The answer, I knew, was the long-cultivated liberal dark money machine.

*

For those of you who haven't heard the term—or who have heard it but don't know what it really means—allow me to make it simple. Dark money is money that streams into the American political system through networks of shell organizations whose donors are not public. It is used primarily to keep the names of the biggest donors out of the press. 501(c)(4) organizations, which are often associated with dark money, have some noble purposes when they are utilized for their intended mission. A key example is the NAACP, which fought to protect its donor list during the civil rights movement to shield supporters from harassment and violence. In *NAACP v. Alabama* (1958), the Supreme Court ruled that the state could not force the NAACP to disclose its donors, recognizing that doing so would put them at risk of intimidation. This principle—that donors should be able to support causes they believe in without fear of retribution—has long been a cornerstone of free association in American politics.

For years, conservative donors faced similar threats, fearing liberal backlash for financially supporting causes they believed in. They turned to dark money as a way to protect themselves from being doxxed, harassed, or targeted by activist groups and the media. I can understand and appreciate donors who wish to remain anonymous in order to advance policy causes they believe in. That's the intent of these committees.

Ironically, given the situation now, it was Democrats who spent years claiming that dark money was a conservative creation being used to subvert democracy. This perception took hold in the wake of key Supreme Court victories for conservative and pro-life groups, which expanded the ability of organizations to engage in political speech without disclosing their donors. Books such as Jane Mayer's *Dark Money* attempted to trace the billions of dollars that flowed into the coffers of political activist groups and super PACs, almost all of which framed dark money as a distinctly Republican issue.

The 2020 election proved otherwise. Democrats, while assailing dark money in public, were quietly building a dark money machine of their own—not to advance policy, but to target democracy itself. Billions of dollars flowed into supposedly nonpartisan organizations in many states, including Missouri. As early as the summer of 2020, we began hearing reports of massive sums of money being funneled into groups whose real purpose was to elect Democrats and oppose President Trump. A great deal of this money came from Mark Zuckerberg, who would soon make headlines for his willingness to censor the speech of Americans on Meta at the behest of the Biden Administration. Before long, these "Zuckerbucks" were flowing freely, always to left-leaning organizations. What had once been a defensive tool for conservatives seeking to protect their identities from political retaliation had been transformed into an offensive weapon by the Left—one designed not to advance ideas, but to manipulate the electoral process itself.

According to a report published by *The Wall Street Journal* in January 2022, it was only in hindsight that we learned that "a nonprofit called the Center for Technology and Civic Life, or CTCL, funded by Mark Zuckerberg . . . gave $350 million to nearly 2,500 election departments in the course of the 2020 campaign. [In May], it posted its 990 tax form for the period, with 199 pages listing grants to support the 'safe administration' of voting amid Covid-19."[3] Although that might sound just fine on its face, the report quotes an analysis by the Capital Research Center showing in Georgia, for instance, "average grants of $1.41 per head in Trump areas and $5.33 in Biden ones. A conservative group in Wisconsin suggests that extra voter outreach funded by CTCL could have boosted Mr. Biden's turnout there by something like 8,000 votes."[4]

In other words, these groups gave money heavily to areas that were going to swing for Biden while pretending that the money was being spread around to everyone. They were trying to help Democrats win, and they were doing their best to hide it. During a deposition for one of our Elias lawsuits, Justin Smith got the chance to investigate some of the money that was being funneled into our election system. After asking a few questions about a $100,000 grant that local election officials had received from the Secretary of State's office—most of which went to buying giant jugs of hand sanitizer and printing signs about social distancing—Justin asked whether any *other* grants were coming in.

According to the transcript of the deposition, the local election official said, "We did just receive notification of a grant award from the Center for Technology and Civic Life." Justin asked how much the grant was for, and the person said:

A: We have not signed it yet. We just received notification about it.

Q: *Do you have any ballpark idea of how much that grant could be worth?*

A: I've had emailed back some questions about it. But the original amount they've offered was something like $600,000. To date, I have not heard back from them yet about the questions that I have about it. So we have not signed it or accepted it yet.

Q: *To make sure I heard you correctly, did you say $600,000?*

A: Yes.

Q: *Are there any conditions for use of this grant to your knowledge?*

A: They are for Covid expenses for elections in 2020. Over and above what the county has budgeted for.

Q: *How did you become aware of this grant?*

A: Twitter.

Q: When did you become aware of it?

A: I think around Labor Day is when they announced it.

Q: Were you able to find information about the grant after you heard about it?

A: Yes, it was tweeted about. I followed the organization on Twitter.

Q: What do you know about the organization?

A: They provide training materials and courses. They do a lot with ballot design, engagement with voters, and recommendations on how to do that better. They also conduct studies.

Q: Was it through your research on Twitter that you were able to learn that this grant could be used for expenses for elections in 2020?

A: The press release noted that it was for this purpose, and it circulated through the county association. When they printed out the interest form, it was a Google form, and it said this was the purpose of the grant. In the application process, they asked what it would be used for.

Q: Do you have any idea on the timing for receiving funds from that grant?

A: No. I literally got the email yesterday afternoon. I heard some other clerks got emails weeks before me, so I don't know why I got mine yesterday afternoon.

As you can see from the reticence of the local election official, the money coming in from CTCL clearly stretched the bounds of what was considered acceptable in our elections. The money amounts to an unprecedented injection of private funding that undermined the principle of impartial election administration.

The presence of money from people like Mark Zuckerberg in our elections has become a hot-button issue, and not only because it arguably helped swing the election for Joe Biden in key districts. The insane amount of dark money that flowed into politics during the 2020 election speaks to just how different things are than they were just a few years ago as it relates to election integrity. The Left is willing to weaponize something that it publicly decries for political gain. According to a report conducted by *The New York Times*, of all places (which did happen to use data collected by the aforementioned Capital Research Center), left-wing groups seriously outspent right-wing ones in the lead-up to election day in 2020. According to this report, which was authored in part by Kenneth P. Vogel, "Spurred by opposition to then-President Trump, donors and operatives allied with the Democratic Party embraced dark money with fresh zeal, pulling even with and, by some measures, surpassing Republicans in 2020 spending. . . . The analysis shows that 15 of the most politically active nonprofit organizations that generally align with the Democratic Party spent more than $1.5 billion in 2020—compared to roughly $900 million spent by a comparable sample of 15 of the most politically active groups aligned with the G.O.P."[5]

One of these groups, according to the report, was called the Hopewell Fund, led by none other than Marc Elias. "His firm at the time," according to the *Times*, "Perkins Coie, was paid $9.6 million by Hopewell, according to tax returns, and another $11.6 million by the Biden-backing Priorities USA nonprofit group."

Obviously, this was never about making sure that everyone had the same opportunities to vote. It was about making sure that *some* people (namely the ones who were going to vote for Joe Biden) were allowed to vote no matter how questionable their ballots were, and that any attempts to secure our elections would be decried as unnecessary, cruel, or even racist. This represented a fundamental change to our election system, and it severely undermined public trust in our government. According to recent data compiled by the Pew Research Center, only 70 percent of Americans are at least "somewhat confident" that our elections will be administered well. While that is up from 62 percent in 2020, it is still far less than the 81 percent who believed it in 2018.[6] And given what we witnessed in 2020, it's no wonder that a majority of those who believe we aren't going to see free and fair elections in this country are Republicans.[7]

Moreover, this didn't used to be a partisan issue. In the early 2000s, the bipartisan Carter–Baker Commission—cochaired by former President Jimmy Carter and former Secretary of State James Baker—recommended ten commonsense safeguards to protect election integrity, including voter ID, signature verification, and limited use of mail-in balloting. Today, however, Democrats cry bloody murder at the mere mention of requiring something as basic as a state-paid ID to vote. According to an October Gallup poll, a staggering 84 percent of Americans support requiring all voters to show photo ID at their polling place. Most industrialized countries around the world enforce similar requirements. But Democrats argue that such measures disproportionately affect voters who may have difficulty locating necessary documents and could discourage participation. Whether intentional or not, the result is the same: looser voting rules that raise concerns about election security.

Missouri was able to beat back all three election-law lawsuit challenges. In other states, citizens weren't so lucky. In the fraught months leading up to the historic 2020 election, as the intelligence community and Big Tech were working overtime to ensure a Biden victory, states such as George, Arizona, and Pennsylvania had their voting laws changed either by settlement or by court order. The Left's victories in court, nearly all of which were paid for by dark money, helped pave the way to Biden's ascendancy to the presidency and were later the basis for many legal challenges to the 2020 election results—one of which I was proud to join on behalf of the people of Missouri.

However, now that the earlier steps in their playbook were complete, the Left moved to shut down the speech of anyone who dared to question what went on during the election of 2020. Cases were thrown out; many people found themselves afraid to speak out. The aftermath of all of this has led to a seismic shift in our elections ever since. Luckily, we learned from our mistakes in 2020 and scored a few key wins in the lead-up to the election of 2024. For instance, Republicans won a decisive victory in Pennsylvania when a court ruled that only properly postmarked ballots would be counted. And we got this done despite claims that anyone who was concerned about illegal voting was an "election denier."

During this time, we were told reliably that voter fraud never happens—and that when it *does* happen, it has no effect on the outcome of the election. Anyone who wants to say otherwise is told to sit down and shut up. During the summer of 2024, we saw plenty of evidence that this is simply not the case. In September 2024, the Oversight Project tweeted a photograph of a voter registration form that a Chinese illegal alien in California had received just two months before the election. According to the tweet, "the form was dual language, consisting of English and Chinese," and it was "an incredibly suspicious development, especially when considering the undeniable links between CCP members, Governor Newsom, the Biden-Harris Administration, and Governor Walz."[8]

As someone who isn't exactly loved by the Chinese Communist Party, I can tell you that when China and Iran—and indeed most foreign nations—attempt to intervene in American elections, they are not doing so on behalf of *my* party. Examples abound. All over the country in advance of the 2024 election, we saw reports that illegal aliens were being registered to vote. In Virginia, according to a recent report from the Heritage Foundation, "more than 11,000 aliens were initially listed on the state's voter roll within the past decade. In New Jersey, at least 616 known aliens ended up in the state's voter registration system just a few years ago. Since 2021, nearly 200 aliens were initially on voter rolls in Arizona."[9]

That October, I joined several of my colleagues in the Senate in signing a letter addressed to U.S. Attorney General Merrick Garland on the matter. The letter demanded answers as to why illegal aliens who attempted to register to vote were not prosecuted.

"We are deeply concerned," we wrote, "by reports of non-citizens registering to vote and voting in federal elections. As of today, there has been no response from you or your Department regarding the inquiry on July 12, 2024, seeking information on efforts undertaken by your Department to enforce laws prohibiting non-citizens voting. Given that the 2024 presidential election is in less than 34 days, your Department's inaction and refusal to provide any information regarding its efforts to promote public trust and confidence in our elections is especially alarming."

Although we requested a response by October 16, we never got one.

*

Looking back at the crucial steps my team and I took during the 2020 election season, I am proud to have provided a model for other states to follow. The most important lesson was to fight back, stand up, and win. We successfully defended all three of the election-related lawsuits filed in Missouri in 2020, including a watershed 5–2 victory on a crucial question of signature verification of mail-in ballots in the Supreme Court of Missouri. In one of the cases, an Obama-appointed federal judge issued an order against us, but in a rare twist, we convinced him to stay his own order pending appeal— essentially admitting that his own order was likely to be reversed on appeal (which it was).

Still, things did not go the way we had hoped. Joe Biden being sworn in as president was yet another surprise in my tenure as Attorney General which affected my role in our system of federalism and threw me into a leading role in some of the most important court dramas in recent American history, and the kitchen was hot. What we saw in Joe Biden and Kamala Harris's first two years was an all-out assault on the rule of law and individual liberty. As it turned out, the Biden-Harris Administration was more aggressive in weaponizing the Administrative State in furtherance of the Left's goals than any administration in American history. I saw it unfolding in real time and was resolute in my role as a defender and in fighting back. We had a republic to save, and the free state of Missouri would be front and center in the fight.

After the 2020 election, I remember my team and the staff at Republican Attorneys General's offices seemed dispirited by the prospect that the new Biden Administration would implement left-wing policies to undermine American strength and security, but there wasn't going to be time to mope around. So, we decided to get ready for some of the fights to come together, The Republican Attorneys General Association (RAGA) was then led by Adam Piper, later Pete Bisbee, and now again by Adam. They were already thinking about how we might take on the Biden Administration. Another key leader in the fights to come that I would lean on was Stephen Miller, a good friend who would go on to found America First Legal then, of course, play a leading role in the Trump 47 White House. But in those dark days in late 2020 and early 2021, that felt very far away. Stephen is loyal and brilliant and was helpful in the early staging of what might lie ahead.

Early on Biden came after Trump's successes. One key area was the energy independence achieved under President Trump. One of Biden's earliest acts in office was to issue an executive order creating a federal working group to ensure that all federal agencies would use the same so-called "Social Cost of Carbon" in their agency rules and calculations. Described by one liberal commentator as "the most important number you've never heard of," the "Social Cost of Carbon" is a method the Left uses to calculate incredibly speculative estimates of the supposed costs of global warming, projected

hundreds of years into the future. These estimates are so speculative that they are based on climate models that purport to predict
the trajectory of world history over the next three hundred years.
Yet these "voodoo" numbers are used to justify job-killing regulations and expensive federal mandates in many industries, resulting
in an enormous "hidden tax" on consumers. This was like implementing the "Green New Deal" without any input from Congress or
the American people, through regulatory fiat.

My office took the initiative in filing, in early March, the first
multistate lawsuit against the Biden Administration—a legal
challenge to the Social Cost of Carbon initiative, arguing that it
violated the Constitution's separation of powers and the Administrative Procedure Act. The lawsuit, which we filed on March
8, 2021, was joined by Arizona, Arkansas, Indiana, Kansas, Mon-
tana, Nebraska, Ohio, Oklahoma, South Carolina, Tennessee, and
Utah. It challenged President Biden's Executive Order 13990, which
unilaterally set new "social cost" estimates for greenhouse gas emissions and mandated that all federal agencies use these values when
implementing regulations. The order sought to justify trillions of
dollars in regulatory costs by assigning speculative, inflated costs
to carbon dioxide, methane, and nitrous oxide emissions—without
congressional approval or proper rulemaking procedures. The Biden
Administration was attempting to dictate sweeping environmental
policy from the White House, bypassing the democratic process and
placing a heavy regulatory burden on businesses, consumers, and
entire industries like agriculture and energy.

We assembled a coalition of thirteen states to sue the Biden Administration, and our friends and allies in Louisiana soon followed
suit with a similar coalition of states to file a second lawsuit. Suddenly,
over twenty states were standing up against the Biden Administration's overreach and fighting back against a regulation that would
have devastated economic growth and cost American jobs.

This first multistate lawsuit was a shot in the arm to the conservative legal movement. It quickly became clear that the Biden Administration's policies were not only deeply unpopular but also blatantly illegal. Many such multistate lawsuits followed. Indeed, our office alone would lead major legal challenges against the Biden Administration's Treasury Department's "Tax Mandate," which attempted to prohibit states that accepted federal Covid-19 relief funds from cutting their own taxes for citizens; its cancellation of President Trump's "Remain in Mexico" policy, which violated federal immigration law and encouraged record-breaking illegal immigration; its unlawful refusal to use appropriated funds to build the border wall, despite Congress already allocating the money for construction; its sweeping vaccine mandates, which attempted to force private businesses, federal contractors, and health care workers to take the Covid-19 shot, regardless of individual choice; its illegal student loan forgiveness, which would have forced blue-collar workers to subsidize the debts of Ivy League theater professors without congressional approval; and its unconstitutional pressure on social media platforms to silence dissenting speech, a brazen violation of the First Amendment.

If this first multistate lawsuit taught us anything, it was that the best defense is a good offense. We had developed a winning legal strategy, one that would be used repeatedly to push back against Biden's unconstitutional overreach.

And we weren't just fighting. We were playing to win.

Chapter 4

CHALLENGING VACCINE
MANDATES

A few days after Joe Biden's vaccine mandates came down in 2021, I entered a large conference room at the iconic Hotel del Coronado with over a dozen other Republican state Attorneys General. We'd all come from our home states, and we all wanted to figure out the best way to beat back these mandates. People around the country were furious, and rightfully so.

After all, Biden had just warned them that his "patience was wearing thin" with people who refused to get vaccinated, sounding more like a TV mob boss than a president of the United States. I had promised the people of my state that I would do something.

And I wasn't the only one.

When you're a state AG, collaboration is key. There's a reason that so many lawsuits filed by states against the federal government include other states as plaintiffs. Filing alongside other states shows unity. It usually gets the federal government's and the courts' attention. Typically, one state or a couple of states will lead a lawsuit and others interested in showing support will either join as co-plaintiffs or jointly file what's called an amicus (friend of the court) brief. Working together allows us to strike with one hammer, so to speak, and gives us the best chance of making an impact.

In the room that afternoon were Republican AGs from all over the United States, top members of their staff, and staff from the Rule of Law Defense Fund, the policy arm of RAGA. Pete Bisbee was now the executive director of RAGA and was excellent. David Johnson was the executive director of the defense fund and was great as well. Between the two of them they helped coordinate our activities in different ways. The organization we all belonged to, RAGA, was immensely helpful to me during my time in office. We were a pretty close group, and there is a certain bond that is formed when you are in the trenches with a colleague. Most of us were pretty likeminded as well. It was a high-caliber group, and I loved serving as vice chairman and later chairman before I had to step down for the U.S. Senate run earlier in 2021. I was proud of the work that we did, and I knew even at the time this new effort we were embarking on would be historic. I was thrilled when Ashley Moody, the bright and effective Attorney General for Florida, joined me in the U.S. Senate.

We were also one of the first national political organization to begin meeting in person again way back in the summer of 2020. The meetings were always dynamic and there is simply no substitute for looking at another human across the table and having a conversation. Typically, these strategy sessions were dynamic and often very collaborative. They often took the form of pitch sessions, during which one AG would stand up and lay out a lawsuit he or she was planning to file. If it seemed like something that could work, other states would sign on. From there we'd have the resources of multiple offices for gathering evidence, sharpening arguments, and working through legal arguments and strategies.

During the meeting in San Diego, everyone was champing at the bit to take on the recent vaccine mandates. Although they had been announced as one big block of tyranny, the mandates Biden was referring to actually included several different rules, all of which applied to different businesses and agencies. There was the mandate from the Occupational Safety and Health Administration (OSHA) that applied to most American businesses, another one for federal employees and contractors, and another for health care workers. My office had spent the past few weeks working with small businesses to show just how damaging vaccine mandates would be—not only in Missouri, but around the country. The enthusiasm in the Hotel del Coronado that day was palpable. We all wanted to act, act quickly, and give ourselves the best chance of success.

This was a time for leadership. The OSHA vaccine mandate, a vaccine mandate that applied to private employers that employed more than 100 employees, would affect somewhere between 75–100 million people. Anticipating this desire to act, my office had already drafted a lawsuit to challenge the OSHA mandate because I wanted to walk into that meeting ready to roll. In addition to having the legal theory worked out, we needed a broader litigation strategy since we knew there might be multiple lawsuits filed because lots of AG wanted to show they were willing to take action.

To do that, we took a page out of the Democrats' playbook to challenge this mandate with a new twist. For years, left-wing groups had been filing complaints in friendly district courts, primarily the Northern District of California, and get a ruling or an injunction that affected the entire country. But in this instance, we decided to not file in one locale but in several jurisdictions. At that meeting, I pitched the idea of filing in multiple circuits, and since we had the OSHA lawsuit ready to go, other offices could use ours as a template and move quickly. This strategy gave us more opportunities for success, but we would only file in jurisdictions we felt had a clear composition of judges who would rule on the law, not just rubber-stamp the Biden-Harris edict. Missouri was the first to file against the OSHA vaccine mandate. In fact, one of our deputy solicitors, Jesus Osete, got up before dawn so we could ensure Missouri was indeed first. So, Missouri led the challenge in the Eighth Circuit, while other states took the lead in the Fifth, Sixth, and Eleventh Circuits. We hoped this approach would avoid a relatively (but increasingly less, thanks to President Trump's appointments) unfavorable Ninth

Circuit and maximize our chances. Ultimately, the Sixth Circuit—where Ohio led—was selected by a judicial panel lottery to hear the consolidated OSHA cases.

In January 2022, the U.S. Supreme Court reviewed the OSHA mandate challenge. In a per curiam opinion, Justice Neil Gorsuch stated, "The question before us is not how to respond to the pandemic, but who holds the power to do so. The answer is clear: Under the law as it stands today, that power rests with the states and Congress, not OSHA."

With this decision, the Court struck down the mandate—a significant victory for the rule of law. This case was a prime example of why the courts matter so much for conservatives. Time and again, liberal administrations have attempted to bypass the legislative process and impose sweeping policies through executive agencies. But the judiciary, especially an originalist-leaning Supreme Court, has reaffirmed that policymaking belongs where the Constitution intended: with the states and Congress, or with the President acting within his clearly defined Article II powers. That's not judicial activism—it's judicial restraint, and it's exactly how our system is *supposed* to work. The courts aren't there to pick winners and losers in policy debates. They're there to ensure that power stays where it belongs.

Nearly simultaneously, Missouri was also the first state to challenge the mandate for health care workers, which we brought before a federal judge in St. Louis. We employed a similar strategy of filing in a number of jurisdictions. We obtained an important district court win from Judge Matthew Schelp in St. Louis. The Eighth Circuit upheld an injunction we obtained to block the mandate. However, the Supreme Court later ruled against us on this mandate in a narrow 5–4 decision, with Justice Brett Kavanaugh joining the majority, stating that the mandate was permissible under the spending powers granted to Congress. I disagreed with the majority, but the mandates were beginning to crumble and were rapidly losing public support. So, while we may have lost that battle, we ultimately won the war against these unconstitutional mandates.

The last major battle involved Biden's vaccine mandate for federal contractors, which would have affected hundreds of thousands of people. Missouri was the first to file in this matter as well. We filed this case in St. Louis and secured an injunction from a federal magistrate. It was a temporary win that would become permanent when the other side surrendered. The Biden Administration initially appealed but later dropped its appeals and rescinded the mandate after ending the Covid-19 emergency on May 11, 2023, granting us another victory.

In addition to these cases, Missouri also joined other Attorneys General in filing amicus briefs against the mandate for military personnel. As we argued, "It is not the role of the federal government to dictate personal health decisions of those who risk their lives for this country." This case, like the others, underscored our commitment to protecting individual liberty against federal overreach. We believed that our military, of all organizations, couldn't afford to tell people they needed to make certain medical decisions if they were going to serve. Throughout all of this, Missouri became the state in the nation most identified with the fight against Joe Biden's Covid tyranny, and I suddenly found myself identified as the lead legal antagonist of the Biden Administration.

Depending on what room I was in, that could be a very good or a very bad thing. Most of the time, it was good. I'd walk down the street and people would shout nice things at me, pumping their fists and telling me to keep fighting for freedom. Sometimes, I'd find myself in a place with scared, masked-up people who didn't like that I was fighting to end pandemic restrictions. But even that wasn't so bad. At least I knew I was doing the right thing, and quite frankly I learned to embrace the fact that I was standing up for people who didn't have the same opportunity to fight back as I did. That gave me a lot of strength.

During another RAGA meeting in Park City, Utah, around this same time, I happened to run into Robert F. Kennedy Jr., who'd come to the conference because he believed that he and the folks at RAGA might have some common ground when it came to excesses of current Covid-related policy and government tyranny in general. It wasn't lost on anyone that he was still a Democrat. When I first ran into him in the hallway outside the ballroom, I recognized him, of course, and he had the Kennedy aura. But he surprised everyone within a five-foot radius by coming up to me, grabbing me by the shoulders, and saying, "You're my hero."

I had to look left and right to make sure there wasn't someone standing behind me. This was a *Kennedy* after all. Although I didn't say what I was thinking—which was *How the hell do you even know who I am?*—I did manage to find out that RFK Jr. happened to have seen a viral press conference I did in St. Louis.

That press conference, which had started with the announcement of a development in a cold case, had ended with an off-the-cuff speech about the tyranny that Joe Biden was attempting to impose on the people of the United States. "If someone says that using fear is good, that is what every tyrant in the history of the world, and every dictator in the history of the world has ever said to accumulate, aggregate and maintain power," I said. "This is America, the freest country in the history of the world, and I don't think we should allow politicians who want to grab power and never let go of it gain it in the first place. People can make their decisions. I believe in freedom, I believe in responsibility. People can make decisions themselves. I don't want to live in some futuristic, dystopian biomedical security state." It ended up becoming one of my most viral speeches—viral enough, as it turned out, to catch the attention of RFK Jr.

For a few minutes, RFK Jr. and I spoke about the state of the country under Joe Biden and Kamala Harris. Like me, he was stunned at how quickly some people had acquiesced to the demands of the Experts™ when it came to this new vaccine. He was also upset that Democrats had seemed to abandon things like the Constitution and free speech. Later, in a small group as we talked further, he brought up the Milgram Experiment. As he began, I recalled it from some coursework or readings from my past. It was obviously relevant for the Covid Times we were living through.

In this experiment, which was conducted at Yale University in the early 1960s by psychology professor Stanley Milgram, participants were instructed to administer electric shocks to a "learner" located on the other side of a wall. The setup included a man in a white lab coat—presumed to be a scientist—who instructed participants to press a button that would deliver shocks to the learner whenever he gave an incorrect answer to a question. Unbeknownst to the participants, the learner was an actor, and the screams of pain they heard were prerecorded. As the experiment progressed, the shocks increased in intensity. Although many participants expressed discomfort and hesitance, they continued to press the button when urged by the authority figure dressed in scientific garb, even as the screams grew louder and more desperate. Eventually, researchers found that a majority of participants were willing to administer what they believed to be extremely painful, even lethal, shocks when instructed by the authority figure in scientific garb.

RFK Jr. was making the point that a lot of damage can be done when someone in authority leads them astray.

The implication was obvious and still haunts me to this day, and one I thought about often during the worst days of the Covid-19 pandemic. I hated watching so many leaders turn into Covid tyrants and pressing others to turn in their neighbors for not doing X, Y, or Z. It was shocking to see fellow Americans screaming at strangers in the street for refusing to wear masks or get vaccinated. It was all pretty chilling. The difference between what we were living through and the Milgram Experiment, of course, was that the people being hurt by Biden's Covid tyranny weren't paid actors. This wasn't for some medical journal or a white paper. People were losing their jobs, friendships, and a real sense of community because so many, particularly on the political Left, were obsessed with conforming to the "current thing" and there was immense power to be had by those pushing it. In fact, thousands would die of despair.

As we've seen, the Left demands total conformity on all things.

No one can step out of line.

*

Looking back on the fight over vaccine mandates today, I'm immensely proud of the work we did. The more we find out about the Covid-19 vaccines and their attendant side effects, the more I thank God we had the foresight to step in and stop the Biden Administration from making them mandatory. That's not to say that I'm against vaccines. But I *am* against government tyranny, and I'm especially opposed to scientists lying to the American people to suit a particular agenda.

Every day, we see evidence of just how much the Experts™ were willing to cover up. According to recent reviews of the scientific literature, Covid vaccines were responsible for an uptick in many diseases, including myocarditis. The severe adverse effects, or SAEs, that came from the Covid-19 vaccines were far worse than other SAEs that got similar vaccines pulled from the market in years past. These issues will rightly be parsed out over time and debated, but for me the central issue was whether the federal government—or a bunch of state and local bureaucrats who'd never been granted authority by the legislatures—could force people to make medical decisions that they didn't want to make. To that, my answer was always no. And I was willing to go fight like hell in court to prove it.

Today, as I go about my work in the United States Senate, I am especially mindful of protecting individual liberty and freedom, in large part because I have seen what happens when we don't—or when we act too slowly. The damage that the people of the United States endured because of the Biden-Harris Administration's forced vaccine mandates has not gone away. For example, more than 8,500 highly trained military men and women lost their jobs, and we had a health care shortage before the mandate was lifted. President Trump has invited them back. But that's a hard sell considering the disrespect shown to them by Joe Biden and his administration. Many good teachers left their profession rather than comply with Biden's unconstitutional mandates. The scars are still visible on every child who was forced to go without quality education during Covid times. Continuing to live in a free country depends on remembering exactly what this strange period was like—the mandates, the public shaming, and the nakedly authoritarian appeals from the Biden White House.

And unfortunately, vaccines weren't even half the battle.

We still had to deal with masks.

Chapter 5

THE LIBERATION GAME

In October 2022, with just weeks to go in a hard-fought campaign for the United States Senate, I boarded a flight from my hometown of St. Louis and headed for Los Angeles. I wasn't looking forward to the trip.

For one thing, I liked campaigning in my home state. This Senate race was my third statewide race in six years. Missouri is a culturally diverse state, and there is a reason why for a very long time it was the ultimate bellwether. The demographics line up with our national demographics pretty well; it has urban centers, suburban, exurban, and rural diffused. Southeast Missouri is a lot like other SEC states, southwest Missouri is more like Texas or Oklahoma, St. Louis faces to the east, Kansas City faces to the west, and northern Missouri is a lot like Iowa. Traveling the state, you get a real sense of where normal folks are in their lives, and the issues relevant in one part of the state may not be as relevant somewhere else. But when you are running for a seat that has national implications, sometimes you travel outside your state to raise money.

The stakes were high in my U.S. Senate race. My opponent, an Anheuser-Busch heiress named Trudy Busch Valentine, was outspending me badly. Adding to the degree of difficulty was the fact that I was being counted on to win my race without any national money from the National Republican Senatorial Committee, which believed the funds could be better spent on tighter races in

Pennsylvania, Arizona, Wisconsin, Nevada, and Georgia. Having won the Republican primary by a convincing margin in a historic (but expensive) twenty-one-person race, I believed we were in good shape. Still, the fundraisers suggested I make one more trip out to the west coast to bring in some additional dollars for television ads before the election.

I had several meetings each day I was there, but one afternoon a couple of them got moved or canceled. So I decided to walk across the street from my hotel to the Santa Monica Pier and take a walk on the beach. I had my AirPods in and was listening to some nineties west coast hip-hop to fully embrace these forty-five minutes or so of peace before I inevitably had to get back on the phone and make some fundraising calls. I have to admit that even with all the state's screwed-up politics, Southern California is beautiful. I remember also wishing my family was with me on the beach that day. They are never very far from my thoughts when I travel. I walked slowly down the beach, watching skateboarders glide past idle surfers and street vendors up on the boardwalk. Everyone around me seemed happy to be outside. The sand felt cool beneath my feet, and the sound of the waves crashing was nice.

Then I saw something strange.

A young couple was walking toward me in beach clothes, their hands clasped. They were average in height and build, both with dark hair. But one thing really stood out.

They were both wearing masks.

At the time, we were more than two years removed from the worst of the Covid-19 pandemic. Rates of infection were lower than they'd ever been. I had managed to make it all the way from my front door in St. Louis to my hotel in Los Angeles (a trip that included two airports, one plane, and a car) without seeing one cloth face mask out in the wild. And now here I was, walking outside in the bright sunshine, staring at two seemingly healthy people in their mid-twenties, masked up like they were standing in a Manhattan hospital corridor in March 2020.

I remember wondering: How the hell did we get here?

In a sense, I knew. The two people walking along the beach in their masks were simply collateral damage of the Left's playbook. These people had probably absorbed all the most apocalyptic warnings from far-left media sources, some of which were *still* telling us that Covid-19 was a never-ending plague that would require masking until the end of time, and those warnings had burrowed deep into their psyches. By the fall of 2022, surveys had revealed troubling spikes in anxiety and depression among young kids and teenagers, a rise that had largely been attributed to the social isolation of the pandemic. Employers were reporting that kids who had come of age during Covid-19 were having much more trouble adjusting to in-person interactions than their peers who'd come of age before the pandemic.

These were the Covid Times. For almost two years, our government had conducted a vast social experiment on the population of the United States, telling everyone that they should fear their friends and neighbors. According to Democrats and the media, other people were simply potential carriers of disease, and seeing their bare faces meant that they didn't care whether you lived or died. That might seem small, but it's those small things that can deeply scar the brains of some people. I couldn't think of any other explanation for why two young, healthy people would still be wearing masks outside two years after the pandemic began.

In part, masks had become a status symbol and an instant way to virtue-signal. It was a way for liberals to declare their belief in the Science™ (which, oddly, they had come to view as a kind of replacement religion). Even today, you might still pass someone on the road wearing a mask all alone in their car, and others still feel the need to cover their faces to show that they have the right political allegiances or that they are morally superior. Others will be doing so because they have serious fears of contracting Covid-19. And others might be wearing a mask for legitimate health reasons.

Pre-Covid, this wasn't a common sight. Now that we've come out the other side of the virus, it's worth asking ourselves why we allowed this to happen in the first place. Masking, after all, didn't need to become a political act. Those who wanted to do it could have done it without attempting to force it on others.

In fact, there was a time when the strongest proponents for masks had an opinion very much like my own.

Once again, we should take a few moments to remember who, what, where, when, and why.

*

Unlike some other states, Missouri never had a statewide mask mandate. Governor Mike Parson announced early on that although he was not anti-mask, he was "anti–mask mandate." His position, as outlined in a tweet from December 2021, was If you want to wear a mask, wear one. However, I do not support government issued mask mandates that infringe on our personal liberties.[1]

I couldn't have said it better myself.

Unfortunately, when you have no mask mandate in a state, it leaves the door wide open for various low-level bureaucrats, following the example of blue-state governors, to try to make their own rules. To these people, personal freedom was not nearly as important as signaling allegiance to a political tribe. None of them seemed able to countenance a world in which they didn't have the right to tell citizens what to wear on their faces, where to go to eat, and what medical decisions they needed to make. In many ways, these Democrat officials were competing to be the wokest and most pro-Covid-restrictions in the Covid era.

So, as the pandemic wore on, we saw some citywide and county-wide mandates pop up. It happened in St. Louis City, St. Louis County, Kansas City, and Jackson County, Missouri. I decided that I'd had enough, and not only because I was born and raised and lived in St. Louis County. In many cases, these officials had initiated mandates without the votes of elected representatives, claiming that the unique emergency of Covid (even one and a half years later) gave them the right to make up authority to force masking. These decisions crushed livelihoods of small business owners and severely limited the ability of people to attend public gatherings, even church, for the simple crime of not wearing a mask. Working quickly, my team and I decided we were going to sue.

And we were going to start in St. Louis County.

The general thrust of the lawsuit was simple. We argued that counties did not have the authority to impose mandates because the state never delegated this authority to its political subdivisions, that is, cities and counties. As we stated in our first filing, which we submitted on the very day the mask mandate went into effect, "St. Louis County and St. Louis City seek expanded government power that has failed to protect Missouri citizens living within their boundaries in the past and is not based on sound facts and data." The suit laid out a series of legal challenges, arguing that the mandates were unconstitutional, exceeded the authority of local governments, violated state law, and were unsupported by clear scientific evidence. The mask mandates, we pointed out, were arbitrary and capricious, particularly for children, who were at a statistically low risk for severe illness from Covid-19. We also argued that the mandates placed a significant burden on personal freedoms and religious liberty, given that they applied even in houses of worship. Additionally, the lawsuit invoked Missouri's recently passed House Bill 271, which explicitly limited the duration of local health orders unless approved by a governing body.

Suits in Kansas City and Jackson County followed, expanding the fight across the state. We prepared for a legal battle, and we sued St. Louis County first. The media lost their minds. It was big news. No other Attorney General in the country was challenging jurisdictions in their own state over mask mandates. The press accused us of politicizing public health. Democratic leaders framed the lawsuit as reckless. Tashara Jones, who was then the mayor of St. Louis, tweeted, Please help us! Our attorney general is literally trying to kill us! But we were standing on solid legal ground, and we were standing up for the fundamental rights of Missourians.

And importantly, in that first lawsuit—against St. Louis County—we won. The judge ruled against the county's attempt to keep its mandate in place, and just like that, a million people had been liberated from Covid tyranny. That victory, and the willingness to stand up and fight back, set the tone for every legal battle that followed. The Covid authoritarians and their media allies were stunned. Local officials scrambled to figure out their next move.

But something even more significant was happening. Our lawsuits and that initial win against mask mandates galvanized the opposition, or the resistance if you will. People felt heard. People who had objected to these mandates for months—who had been ridiculed and dismissed—finally had someone willing to fight for them. I remember getting a voicemail from a longtime friend from college saying, "I was willing to go along with this bullshit for a while, but no more. Let me know what I can do to help."

St. Louis County, desperate to regain control, tried to push through another mask mandate by holding a vote. That vote failed—even though Democrats held the majority on the council. The legal victory had sent a shock wave through the system. We had caused quite a stir and quite a disruption. Eventually, St. Louis County re-issued another mask mandate, as did the other jurisdictions. But we didn't back down. We kept up the legal pressure, filing additional challenges and forcing officials to justify every order they tried to impose. The momentum was on our side.

There were many hurdles along the way. As national case counts rose and fell, different city- and county-level bureaucrats attempted to reinstate the mandates. But every time they did, my office filed suit against them, arguing that the mandates were "prohibited orders" under the law. Repeatedly, we cited a Missouri law that states: "A political subdivision shall not issue a public health order of general applicability during a time other than a state of emergency that directly or indirectly closes an entire classification of businesses, churches, schools, or other places of gathering or assembly for a period of time longer than 21 days in a 180-day period. Such orders may be extended more than once upon a two-thirds vote of the political subdivision's governing body."

This was now a two-sided argument, and our communications team—led by Marianna Deal, one of the country's best communications professionals, whom I had convinced to join me in the Attorney General's Office, and Chris Nuelle, my gifted and hardworking AG press secretary whom I would later make my Senate communications director—was hitting on all cylinders. We would end up challenging every one of the mandates in every city and county and every city and county ended up dropping every single one of them. Our playbook was now coming into view for more people to see.

As I said during a press conference shortly thereafter, the proposed mandates and vaccine passports were simply a way for the government to acquire, aggregate, and maintain power. "If you're vaccinated and you want to wear six masks while jogging around Forest Park for hours, this is America, and you're certainly free to do that. But the actions I've taken in court are to prevent government from attempting to impose their will on the people of Missouri."

All this was not without some serious political risk. In fact, many advised me against this course of action. If you had a time machine and went back to those critical days, the public sentiment was not what it is now. Many liked the forced masking, and if you were on the fence—although that population was dwindling—maybe you just said, "What's the big deal?" Maybe it was the contrarian in me or the "defender" DNA I talked about earlier. Whatever it was, I decided to dig in, stand up, and fight. I wasn't going to back down no matter what pressure came from the other side.

But once again, this wasn't a problem that was confined to local municipalities in St. Louis and Kansas City. At some point, we knew we were going to have to take on the federal government.

It was only a question of when.

Fortunately, that question wasn't difficult to answer. As soon as we got word that Joe Biden and Kamala Harris would attempt to mandate masks for children, we knew exactly what to do.

*

Sometimes, when you're trying to get things done via the American legal system, you have to be prepared to wait. Over the years, I've had cases sit on the docket for years, the paperwork gathering digital dust as we all sit around waiting for something to happen. In part, this is by design. American courts are set up to allow both parties in lawsuits to make the best and most complete versions of their arguments. That takes time, and it *should* take time. I often found that by the time things got moving in the courts, the issue I was trying to tackle would have resolved itself (as happened with the municipal and county mask mandates in the last chapter).

Every once in a while, though, you get a quick win.

That's what happened to my team at the Missouri AG's office in late 2021 when we filed suit against the Biden-Harris Administration for attempting to mandate masks and vaccines in the federal Head Start program. The Head Start program has been around for decades and was well intended, but it had mixed results.

In Missouri, where approximately 12.5 percent of families live below the federal poverty line, the Head Start program has been widely utilized. However, studies have shown mixed outcomes regarding its effectiveness. But one thing we knew for sure was that, for families that utilized the program who were actually working in person somewhere, there was no way for a parent whose child had been told that they were no longer welcome at the program to make other arrangements.

In some cases, the kids at Head Start were the children of the essential workers who had never been able to simply work from their laptops at home. They were the kids of food delivery workers, factory workers, and other blue-collar tradespeople who needed to be somewhere between eight and five to keep the country running and their families fed. Many of these people couldn't afford to keep their kids home if they happened to disagree with the requirements that their kids wear masks during their programs.

And just in case I haven't made this clear enough already, these were kids we were talking about—the one group of Americans who faced the lowest risk from Covid-19. Yet they were still forced to mask up and, in many cases, get vaccinated as a condition of attending school. This wasn't about "following the science." The Biden-Harris Administration and its allies ignored data showing that children were at minimal risk and pushed mandates anyway. All they were concerned about was claiming the supposed moral high ground, even if they didn't care who they hurt to get there. Firing workers for refusing the shot was bad enough—but preventing their kids from attending school for the same reason was indefensible.

So, we decided to take that power back.

In late December 2021, I joined a multistate lawsuit that

challenged the mask and vaccine mandates for Head Start kids, arguing that they were "arbitrary and capricious," and that Biden had bypassed Congress by imposing them. We were sure to include data about how masks had been shown to hinder childhood development—which was, after all, the main point of the Head Start program in the first place.

The first page of the complaint read:

The Biden Administration has quadrupled down on its lawless mandates. Facing a barrage of court orders enjoining its first three vaccine mandates, the Administration has not begun to rethink its "sledgehammer" approach. . . . Instead it enacted a new Mandate materially similar to—and in some ways more draconian than— its first three. The Head Start mandate applies to all preschool programs funded by the federal Head Start program, regulating hundreds of thousands of staff, volunteers, and preschool students nationwide. It forces vaccinations on staff, volunteers, and other in contact with the Head Start students and forces masks on everyone age two and up. It includes few exceptions, is projected to lead to tens of thousands of Head Start agency staff losing their jobs, and will cause programs to close or reduce capacity—achieving the very opposite result of its purported goal. The Department of Health and Human Services enacted the Head Start Mandate 82 days after announcing its intent to do so, but made the mandate effective immediately and (like the other three federal vaccine mandates) bypassed notice and comment.

Once again, the language and the stakes were clear from the beginning. Anyone who logged on and read the complaint could see that the mandate, if enacted, would lead to trouble for hundreds of thousands of people.

One of those people, as it turned out, was U.S. District Judge

Terry Doughty, who immediately granted an injunction blocking the mandate in January 2022. In a matter of weeks (which happened to include Christmas and New Years), the mandate was gone. Today it stands as a testament to what can be achieved using the legal system as long as you coordinate with the right people, state your claims clearly, and strike at the right time.

Unfortunately, the fight against mask mandates for the older kids in Missouri would not be quite so simple.

But it was a fight I was more than willing to take on.

Chapter 6

MASK MANDATES IN
LOCAL SCHOOLS

On August 10, 2021, the streets of Jefferson City, Missouri, were crowded with people. Bunting and flags lined the streets. A big parade streamed by in the streets. After more than a year of lockdowns and social distancing restrictions, it seemed we were finally getting back to some sense of normalcy.

The occasion was the bicentennial of Missouri entering the Union, which occurred in August 1821. Back then, most of what people knew about Missouri came from reports sent back by Daniel Morgan Boone, the son of Daniel Boone, who described it, according to the historian David McCullough, as a "New Eden." The people who first came to settle the land were largely of Scotch-Irish descent. As McCullough writes in his biography of the famous Missourian Harry Truman, these people "saw themselves as the true Americans. Their idol was Andrew Jackson, Old Hickory of Tennessee, 'One-man-with-courage-makes-majority' Jackson, the first president from west of the Alleghenies.... Their trust was in the Lord and common sense. That they and their forebears had survived at all in backwoods Kentucky—or earlier in upland Virginia and the Carolinas—was due primarily to 'good, hard sense,' as they said, and no end of hard work."[1]

My ancestors arrived from Germany in the first real immigrant wave after Missouri became a state, all the way back in the 1840s, when Missouri was as far west as you could go. And like many from the Show Me State, I retain a certain Missouri independent streak. Anyone walking through the Supreme Court building in Jefferson City that day would have seen it on full display. On that day, some officeholders held receptions, but many did not as they wanted to avoid gatherings. Almost every one of these receptions required masks. Not mine. Context is important here as well. State law requires the Attorney General's Office to be located in the Supreme Court Building, across the street from the Missouri State Capitol. Thus we were tenants in a building larger than just our office. In that building, mask mandates were strictly enforced. My office, in contrast, was dubbed "the freedom zone," where attendees were free to go maskless, and they didn't have to worry about shouting at one another from six feet apart.

It wasn't just the bicentennial celebration. For the past few months, as the Covid cases wound down and our lawsuits against mask mandates made their way through the courts, my team and I practiced what we preached. We worked mostly in person, and we didn't wear masks while doing it.

Somehow, we were all still alive.

Little did I know that we had a guest that day. That afternoon, a reporter from *The Atlantic* named Kathy Gilsinan walked through the halls of the Supreme Court building, stopping every few feet to ask people about me. She would later talk to others in the state government, as well as people from my church and a couple of other stops along the way in life. She had emailed my team a list of questions, but I had declined to speak to her on the assumption that she was going to write a hit piece about me. It turned out that I was right. Sort of.

The profile that resulted from her interviews ran in *The Atlantic* under the headline "Missouri's Unmasked Avenger." The artwork showed me standing proudly against a backdrop that included washed-out images of a mask, a government building, and a map of my home state of Missouri. I had it printed out and hung in my office almost as soon as it hit the magazine's website.

The reporting was tough, but fair. Kathy interviewed some of my old political rivals and detractors. But I didn't mind. Politics is a tough business, and I had developed pretty thick skin. Interestingly, Kathy and I have become friendly in the years since she wrote the profile. I ran into her at the Missouri State Fair in August 2024, and I did have to thank her for making me look cool in a national publication, although that was not *The Atlantic*'s goal at the time.

Looking back, I'm amazed at the portrait she managed to paint of the space right outside my office. If nothing else, it stands as a monument to just how crazy the world went in the aftermath of Covid-19.

"There's a particular spot in Jefferson City, Missouri," it reads, "where you can walk a few yards and pass through three different sets of masking rules. Struggling against the heavy wooden doors of the state-supreme-court building and stepping through, you leave the zone of the city and county recommendations—mask when you can't keep distance—and enter a space where masks are required by order of the court. From there, you can peer through a glass door into a government office, a parallel pandemic universe where no one can tell you what to put on your face—and where trying to do so is a form of government overreach and social control."

I couldn't have put it better myself, and so I won't try.

I'm fully aware, of course, that this was meant to be insulting, or at least flippant. But at the time, I was willing to take a little ridicule from the legacy media to stand up for the principles of freedom and individual liberty. Anyone who wanted to wear a mask in my office was free to do so. But telling anyone what to do in this regard was a bridge to far. To me, that just seemed like "good, hard sense," as my ancestors might have put it.

What the reporter from *The Atlantic* didn't know, of course, was that I had no intention of stopping with the 350 or so people who worked in my office, or with the city of St. Louis or St. Louis County, Kansas City, or Jackson County. By the end of that summer, we had learned that more than sixty school districts were planning to implement mask mandates for kids when they returned to school at the end of August. If these mandates went into effect, children as young as four or five years old would be forced to wear masks at all times while on school property. Any children who chose not to wear masks for personal reasons would be sent home, putting those children even further behind in school than they'd been after the disastrous lockdowns of the 2020–21 school year.

In an email that went out to parents in Columbia, Missouri, a district that includes 19,000 students and 3,000 employees on 42 campuses, a representative from the school district wrote, "Wearing masks indoors is one mitigation strategy that will provide an additional layer of protection to keep all students and staff safe and in school. We want to start the year together, in person, and do our best to keep it that way."[2] The email also noted that kids would be required to wear masks regardless of their vaccination status.

In part, I opposed these bans so vehemently because they made no scientific sense. For almost a year, we had known full well that the Covid-19 virus didn't make children any sicker than other seasonal viruses, nor did they die from it or transmit it to their parents at rates higher than the annual flu. Even then, studies had shown that kids were nearly twice as likely to die from a dog attack as from contracting the virus at school. Since the beginning of organized schooling, kids had been dealing with other viruses such as the flu and chickenpox without masks, and they had managed just fine. Just because social media companies routinely banned people for pointing this out didn't mean it wasn't true.

There was simply no measurable benefit to kids wearing masks. And study after study showed that masking young children was at best unnecessary and at worst disruptive to their physical and mental well-being. The data was becoming so clear that not even the vastest censorship complex in human history could keep it hidden. Like other studies before and since, a study conducted by the Harvard School of Public Health in 2022 found that about 40 percent of parents surveyed believed that masking had seriously harmed their kids. More than half of parents surveyed said that masks weren't necessary to protect their kids.

School is for learning. But it also involves social interaction. It's where kids are supposed to get the hang of making friends, speaking with their peers, and working with them to accomplish goals, and that simply can't happen when everyone's faces are covered by blue fabric. But mask mandates persisted because no one wanted to be seen as disrupting the status quo. Teachers' union leaders wanted to virtue-signal and use the virus as leverage for as long as possible—in part, at least, because they didn't want to get back into the classroom. Many school administrators were even worse—either because of fear or a reflexive desire to fit into the groupthink, or both. But the Education Cabal had spoken, and no one dared question it. It was going to take someone with a strong contrarian streak who wasn't afraid of taking the heat to stop the madness.

Luckily, I had just such a streak, as some of my teachers and professors would likely attest. Plus, I happened to have the law on my side.

*

As discussed in Chapter 5, Governor Mike Parson had promised early on that there would be no state mandates, and he had kept his word despite immense pressure from teachers' unions and other Covid obsessives.

But the absence of a state mandate left a lane wide open for liberal mayors and other left-wing institutions to step in and try to make their own rules. St. Louis tried to institute its own mask mandate in July 2021, which fell apart shortly after we filed a lawsuit against them. Other cities had tried the same thing, with little success. Early on, in the absence of information, individuals had been advised to take certain actions, but we were now a year and a half into this. We knew a lot more, and there was now this "end all, be all" Covid shot.

When it came to mask mandates in schools, though, I didn't understand them at all. Either these people were being willfully ignorant about the risk that Covid-19 posed to children—or, as they might put it, failing to "trust the science"—or they truly didn't understand why what they were doing was wrong. To me, it didn't matter either way. Forcing kids to wake up every morning and pull cloth over their faces (or face expulsion) just so a bunch of left-wing adults could feel good about themselves wasn't going to happen in the state of Missouri. In fact, according to the law, it *couldn't* happen in the state of Missouri.

For a brief refresher in Civics 101, it's important to note that the states created the federal government to have *limited* powers, and counties, local municipalities, and school districts are political *sub-divisions* of the state. In a state, the authority to make laws comes from the people through their elected representatives or by direct initiative petition/referendum. Given that the state legislature had never delegated the authority to school districts—which were po-litical subdivisions of the state—to enact group quarantine policies or mask mandates, any action to do so would be illegal. Moreover, on November 23, 2021, a judge declared that health authorities had "grown accustomed to issuing edicts and coercing compliance. It is far past time for this unconstitutional conduct to stop."

Shortly thereafter, I sent legal notices to all health authorities *and* school districts notifying them that mask mandates were illegal and that they should cease and desist from creating or maintaining such policies.

"Under Missouri law," it said, "public health authorities and school districts do not have the authority to impose mask mandates or other public health orders without proper delegation from the state legislature. Any continued enforcement of such mandates is illegal and must cease immediately."

Then I waited.

Because of our pressure, many school districts backed down in December 2021 and announced that they would lift mask mandates immediately or upon return from Christmas break. However, many districts reimposed their mandates by claiming the holidays had caused a spike that necessitated a return to masks. In January 2022, at the peak of the Omicron wave in Missouri, we sued forty-five school districts with parents as co-plaintiffs. We also quietly sued a few more who imposed mandates to put our total over fifty. This was a massive undertaking, but it was necessary. Among the districts we targeted were St. Louis City, St. Louis County school districts (including and especially my own kids' districts), Springfield, Columbia, and Kansas City area school districts. Here's one of the press releases we issued at the time:

> As we've made clear from the beginning, the power to make health
> decisions for their children should be in the hands of parents, not
> bureaucrats. Masking children all day in school is ineffective,
> and these endless pandemic restrictions lead to lasting, negative
> psychological impacts on children and teens. This is a fight worth
> fighting, and I'm not going to back down.

Some districts backed down immediately, which I was happy to see. But for the most part, the letters did nothing but inflame tensions that had been building between my office and school bureaucrats for months. And, as I have found over the course of my time in public service, there is nothing more irritating than a bureaucrat with an ax to grind. Speaking from the White House press briefing room shortly after I filed my initial lawsuit, press secretary Jen Psaki said, "We've seen, including recently I think today or yesterday in Missouri, additional steps taken that in our view put more kids at risk. The president thinks that's completely unacceptable."

From there, all hell broke loose.

Almost every day, school administrators were quoted in local newspapers accusing me of putting our kids in danger. The articles usually ran without the real "fact-checks" pointing out that Covid-19 posed virtually no risk to children. Instead, the new breed of Fact Checkers™ and "verify teams" popped up to affirm the establishment narrative. The executive director of the Missouri School Boards Association told *The Missouri Independent*, "No one likes to wear masks. But what we dislike more than wearing masks is our students and teachers getting sick and having to go virtual."

As usual with the Covid tyrants on the left, these quotes always seemed to carry a hint of a threat. *Do what we say*, they seemed to be telling kids and their parents, *or you'll suffer the consequences*. It was just the latest of many examples of what happens when people get a little bit of power and believe they're in the right. All over Missouri, and the United States, formerly quiet liberal people began turning in their neighbors for having barbecues with too many people or failing to wear six masks while they were outside jogging. It became abundantly clear to me how authoritarian movements spread. For some people, having power can feel good. For some, turning on your neighbors (like snitching on a classmate) feels good, especially when you do it in service of something you believe is right. And even when it doesn't feel good, many people tend to defer to authority because it's comfortable. Anyone who doubts this need only read up on the Milgram Experiment, conducted in 1961 and discussed earlier, in which test subjects were convinced to administer what they believed to be harmful shocks to people simply because a man with a clipboard and white coat told them to.

There were a few bright spots. I couldn't help but laugh, for instance, when Mayor Bill de Blasio of New York set up a "snitch line" for Covid-19 violations only to have it inundated with opposition messaging. I can only hope that the tip line set up by then-Governor Tim Walz of Minnesota received similar messages. But for the most part, the tendency of government bureaucrats to turn friends and neighbors against one another simply to advance their own political agendas was downright chilling.

So, my office decided to set up a "tip line" of our own.

Only this time, it would be a portal for parents whose children were still being forced to wear masks in school. Instead of turning people in to suppress their rights, we would open a portal up to protect their rights from suppression. The symmetry was exquisite. All parents had to do was log onto our website and they would be able to submit complaints—anonymous or signed—directly to the Attorney General's Office. I thought of it as my way of using the Left's own tactics against them.

And it worked.

As soon as the portal went live in December 2021, the messages came pouring in. We got our fair share of hateful notes from Covid obsessives, of course, which we had come to expect over the past few months. But my highly capable assistant Megan Werdehausen and the rest of the team including Morgan Corder dutifully read every line of the messages; it didn't matter what they said.

We learned quickly that the situation on the ground was far worse than we'd thought. In St. Louis, a student was made to sit in isolation for refusing to wear a mask. In Kansas City, teachers enforced mask-wearing by withholding recess from noncompliant students. One student in the Columbia Public Schools system wrote in and said, "I have tried to not wear my mask several times today and every time I get told I have to put one on. I have just put one on to keep myself from being sent home but they are still REFUSING to follow the fact that what they are doing is illegal. Please make it CLEAR to Dr. Yearwood and the BOE that they cannot do this anymore! Remove him along with anyone who refuses to follow this if you can. Enough is enough for us students."

Parents across the state were outraged. A parent from the Fox C-6 school district described how her daughter, placed on a so-called "modified quarantine" after being deemed a close contact of a positive case, was publicly shamed by being forced to eat a segregated lunch in the small gym of her high school. "She was made to sit on the stage at one table, with one chair on the entire stage in front of all her peers," her mother wrote. "I am very upset by the ridiculous rules that go against the Cole County ruling for the state of Missouri."

In Springfield, a mother of a deaf student explained how mask policies made it impossible for her son to communicate effectively in school. "My son is Deaf and wearing a mask directly impacts his ability to communicate clearly," she wrote. "I have tried to work with the school and district to make an exemption for the Deaf, and even after stating how it is inequitable and affects our DHH students differently than their hearing peers, I was ignored and nothing has been done." She explained how both masks and shields disrupted the fluency of ASL, making it harder for deaf students to learn.

The problem extended beyond just masking—it was about punishing noncompliance. A parent from Wentzville described how her child was given a modified quarantine order that forced him to wear a mask all day at school. Yet, absurdly, the same school district banned him from the after-school care program his family had been paying for years to use. "Now I am paying extra for a program that my son is banned from using," she wrote. "I'm also forced to take off from my job in order to get him on the bus. This is all because of Wentzville School District and the Chautauqua program singling out my child, who is not even sick. This is completely ludicrous and needs to stop."

In the end, we received more than 7,500 similar complaints from parents all over Missouri, and we made sure to follow up on each one. This took a great deal of work, but it was necessary to enforce the law.

*

To this day, when I attend events or even when people see me in grocery stores at home in Missouri, people will come up and thank me for fighting against mask mandates in schools. Parents tell me that it was good, especially during those dark times, to have someone fighting for them. Looking back, I've come to realize that in public service, people want to know you'll listen to them and use whatever power you have to fight the system on their behalf. Many in the legacy media claimed the work that my office did to push back against the Left's increasingly radical Covid restrictions was nothing more than a series of publicity stunts. I certainly knew it would get coverage, but that wasn't my motivation. I was fighting for these kids, including the ones sent home because they stood up and refused to wear a mask. I was fighting for the underdogs in this fight and against the adults who should have known better. I think about the small but significant improvements in the school experience that these kids were able to have because we were willing to fight for them.

In fact, just a few months into my new job as a U.S. Senator, I welcomed a group of college-aged interns to Capitol Hill. They came into my office for a quick visit and pictures. I usually ask what their name is and where they are from. While doing so a young woman said, "You sued my high school when you were Attorney General."

Oh boy, I thought. Here we go.

Before I could say anything, the student said, "Thank you."

I posted about the interaction on social media and of course the Left couldn't believe it, they had thought that I made the story up. They've never come to grips with the fact they were *the establishment*; they were *the machine* and it was conservatives raging against it.

As it turned out, most people I ran into during the school masking debate—and especially since then—have been firmly on my side. Many just didn't want to say it, for fear that they'd be socially ostracized by the mask police on the Left. The comment I get the most is "Thanks for standing up for us and our kids when no one else would." As usual, standing up for what I believed was right wasn't always the popular thing to do at the time. Looking back, I am really proud that my team and I were able to help hundreds of thousands of kids regain some sense of normalcy during an insane period for them, and for this country in general.

Every time I see that "Unmasked Avenger of Missouri" headline on the wall of my office, I think about what it feels like to take a stand against government when taking a stand against the government is not a popular thing to do.

And if history is any indication, I'm going to do it a whole lot more before I'm done.

Part II

Uncovering a Vast Censorship Enterprise

Chapter 7

MISSOURI V. BIDEN:
THE MOST IMPORTANT
FREE SPEECH CASE IN
AMERICAN HISTORY

In a plain conference room on the campus of the National Institutes of Health's headquarters in Bethesda, Maryland, about ten lawyers sat at a table, tapping their pens and waiting for Dr. Anthony Fauci to show up.

It was November 2022. I had just been elected to the United States Senate. In a matter of hours, my calendar had gone from nothing but campaign speeches and fundraising dinners to endless meetings about how to set up my new Senate office. In perhaps my last significant act as Attorney General, my office would get an opportunity that was almost as rare as a complete sentence by President Joe Biden. We would sit across from Dr. Anthony Fauci and ask him questions under oath, and Dr. Fauci would be legally obligated to answer.

The deposition had come about as a result of a lawsuit called *Missouri v. Biden*, in which I and Jeff Landry, then–Louisiana Attorney General and now governor, alleged that the federal government had colluded, coordinated, and coerced social media companies to censor the speech of American citizens. At the time it was filed, the suit was the first of its kind. It was panned by liberal critics as a lawsuit filed to garner attention that only fed into "conspiracy theories."

The Biden-Harris Administration had become increasingly brazen in their language, noting that they were working with social media companies and "flagging" posts they believe spread "dangerous misinformation" or "disinformation." They had even created a "Disinformation Governance Board," headed by the "Mary Poppins" of censorship, Nina Jankowicz. Something had to be done. Our lawsuit would eventually peel back the onion and expose the most egregious censorship in American history—on a scale never seen before. Never before had someone gathered this much clear evidence that Joe Biden, Kamala Harris, and various federal agencies had stifled the free speech of Americans, clearly violating the First Amendment of the Constitution. Under the guise of a public health emergency, the Biden-Harris Administration had silenced anyone who dared question what the Experts™ said, even when those utterances turned out to be false. The federal government had pushed Twitter to ban former *New York Times* reporter Alex Berenson for questioning vaccine mandates, and pushed Facebook and Instagram to ban Robert F. Kennedy Jr. They had even pressured Facebook to squelch a video of Tucker Carlson raising concerns about vaccine side effects on his show.

But that wasn't all.

Normally in a lawsuit seeking injunctive relief, that is, getting the government to stop doing something, the plaintiff would seek a temporary restraining order/preliminary injunction very early in the case. The discovery phase comes later. I knew that the allegations we were making would be denied by the government officials, widely criticized, and historic. Therefore, I needed evidence early to shore up the case. So we asked for discovery early, and the judge granted our request. The result was reams and reams of emails, text messages, and other documents. And what we found was shocking.

It turns out the Biden-Harris Administration had gone far beyond what was previously known in the realm of censorship. And it wasn't just about the finer points of the Covid-19 virus. At the behest of some of the highest-ranking government officials in the country, some of the biggest social media companies in the world had censored speech on topics such as the Covid lab-leak theory, the Hunter Biden laptop story, the efficacy of masks, and much more. During the discovery phase, we learned—and later put on the record— that it wasn't just one or two officials who were working with social media companies to censor American voices. It was a Leviathan of government officials and agencies more appropriately dubbed a vast censorship enterprise. This case cut to the very core of what it means to be an American and what we believe in this country: that the federal government should not be censoring the speech of Americans. And they don't get to do an end run around the Constitution by having social media companies do it for them.

Now, just six months after the case was filed and as our discovery efforts continued, we had a scheduled deposition with Dr. Anthony Fauci. It was only the second deposition he was ever forced to sit for. Despite several attempts to shake us off, the man was finally about to sit down with my solicitor general, John Sauer, who would lead the deposition. Other lawyers were present, including myself, Jeff Landry, the Louisiana Attorney General, and others from my team, including Justin Smith and Todd Scott. We had worked hard on what questions to ask, and in what sequence, to limit the opportunities for Fauci to wriggle out of things or pretend he didn't recall certain details. Our main objective was to present him with clear evidence of his role and get him on the record either admitting to them or lying about them. The stakes, as usual, were high.

The mood in the room shifted as Dr. Fauci entered, flanked by a small legal team. I'm sure he did not find it amusing that my friend Jeff Landry had placed a copy of *The Real Anthony Fauci*, by Robert F. Kennedy Jr., on the table in front of him. I'm sure he found it even less amusing when John Sauer caught him in lie after lie in a methodical legal takedown. For the next several hours, he squirmed, dodged, insinuated that he *was* the Science™, then suddenly claimed he couldn't remember anything at all.

This is why conservatives should love discovery. It's one of the most powerful tools for uncovering what institutions would rather keep hidden. In the face of public statements, spin, and carefully managed narratives, discovery forces the truth into the light. Fauci may have been treated as untouchable by the media, but in a deposition he had no choice but to answer—or refuse to answer—questions under oath. And when someone says "I don't recall" 174 times and claims they can't remember or can't recall 212 times, it says more than they realize.

But before we get to what he actually said (or the other blockbuster depositions that occurred as a result of *Missouri v. Biden*), I should say a little about the origins of the case and why it mattered so much to me.

*

When I was in law school at Saint Louis University—the first law school west of the Mississippi—I probably read thousands of pages of case law and dry analysis thereof. Every day brought more and more reading and ultimately with it a way to analyze cases, issues, and problems. But English common law, a relatively new lexicon for me as the first person in my family to go to college out of high school, let alone law school, was a bit dry.

Every once in a while, though, I would encounter an opinion by someone who wrote with verve and a real sense of literary style. These pages would be filled with beautiful language and fascinating stories from historical context. The most prominent author of these opinions was Justice Antonin Scalia, who served on the Supreme Court from 1986 until he died in 2016. During that time,

Justice Scalia pioneered a legal theory known as originalism, which he pointed out (correctly) was the primary method of constitutional interpretation until the early twentieth century, when the country began a serious lurch toward the left and away from reality. For my generation, Justice Scalia and later Justice Clarence Thomas would provide inspiration and the intellectual horsepower to counter the Left's decades-long dominance of the legal zeitgeist.

As he once put it in an essay, this theory held simply that "the provisions of the Constitution have a fixed meaning, which does not change (except by constitutional amendment): they mean today what they meant when they were adopted, nothing more and nothing less." In this he was opposed to the notion of a "living Constitution," which (to quote him again, because why not?) holds that "the Constitution *changes*; that the very act which it once prohibited it now permits, and which it once permitted it now forbids." To those who believed in this theory of a "living Constitution," which had become the de facto method of statutory interpretation by the Left by the time I got to law school in the late 1990s, the Constitution should change with the times. If it meant that, it meant nothing.

In the early 1970s, a left-leaning Supreme Court used this theory to create a right to abortion that never existed in the Constitution. As Justice Samuel Alito wrote in the *Dobbs* decision from 2022, "*Roe v. Wade* was on a collision course with the Constitution the moment it was decided." *Roe* had been decided by nine unelected judges in one fell swoop. The abortion question was always meant to be decided by the states and legislatures—by the people. For a long time this was not a controversial view. It only became that way when the Left just wanted to get its way—process be damned. There are countless examples of the long-liberal court deciding case law to meet policy goals. The Left wanted their liberal justices to act as superlegislators. It was the ultimate trump card. This is offensive to our system of checks and balances and the role of the court within our constitutional structure. The nebulous "penumbras" were often cited by the Supreme Court as a reason to make things up. The law didn't matter. Neither did the actual text of the Constitution. All that mattered was the present moment, and whatever the Democrats wanted to shove through the courts. Anything that was deemed to be important enough entitled them to a new precedent or justices ignoring the plain language of the Constitution or statutes to get their way.

Originalists like Justice Scalia understood that this is not how the law is supposed to work. Unlike the legislative and executive branches, the judicial branch is supposed to exist *outside* politics. The Constitution interpreted by judges and argued over by lawyers doesn't change because people don't like it. It doesn't even change when a *majority* of people don't like it. It is what it is. As Justice Robert H. Jackson put it in his majority opinion in *West Virginia Board of Education v. Barnette* in 1943, "the very purpose of a Bill of Rights was to withdraw certain subjects from the vicissitudes of political controversy, to place them beyond the reach of majorities and officials and to establish them as legal principles to be applied by the courts. One's right to life, liberty, and property, to free speech, a free press, freedom of worship and assembly, and other fundamental rights may not be submitted to vote; they depend on the outcome of no elections."[1]

Moreover, the job of a good judge should be to interpret the law as it is written—not as they'd like it to be written—and certainly *not* to figure out how the law might be twisted to bring about a desired political outcome. Justice Scalia, for example, was famous for surprising his critics by ruling in favor of supposedly "liberal" outcomes when he believed that the law required it. One famous example is *Texas v. Johnson*, when Scalia joined four left-leaning justices to hold that the First Amendment protects the right to burn the American flag in protest. Scalia said that, after that decision, when he came home his wife, Maureen, was humming "She's a Grand Old Flag" to protest his decision.

So, naturally, as I watched the Biden Administration trample on the First Amendment in the name of a "national emergency," I was taken aback. It is also worth recounting why it was so important to our founders that speech never be censored by the government.

Long before the Revolutionary War, the colonists had witnessed the oppression of speech. During the fraught years leading up to that war, in fact, the British government prosecuted Americans more than 1,200 times for "seditious libel," that is, even *truthful* speech criticizing the government. Laws from the king and his minions prohibited criticism of the government, and specific government officials. The king believed that criticism of his policies could inflame the public against the government. Some of these prosecutions directly cited the possibility that inflammatory speech might cause war to break out. Even then, it seems, tyrannical governments knew how to oppress people using the guise of a national emergency.

Some prosecutions, however, appear to have involved little more than sensitive feelings being hurt. For example, one woman faced prosecution for calling the governor and his team "a parcel of pitiful beggarly curs." Another man faced prosecution for calling a judge a "pitiful, lousy rascal." At the turn of the eighteenth century, criticism like this could be punished by large fines, public whippings, and even imprisonment. I can only imagine how busy the royal government would have been if social media had existed back then. The British government would have had to build new courthouses to try all the colonists who called the king names or openly discussed the need for revolution.

Given what they had endured under British colonial rule, the American people made free speech one of their main issues as the Revolutionary War approached. Colonial grand juries began refusing British requests to issue indictments for criticizing the government. Colonial juries acquitted individuals accused of speaking out against the Crown. In one famous incident, the trial of John Peter Zenger in 1735, a colonial jury acquitted a printer charged with seditious libel for criticizing the royal government. Thomas Paine and others rallied colonists with pamphlets making the case against the king and for freedom. The new right of freedom of speech was not easily won. Signers of the Declaration of Independence risked their lives, their fortunes, and their sacred honor; many paid dearly for their act of so-called treason against King George. General George Washington and his ragtag army suffered through starvation, disease, and bitterly cold winters until they triumphed over what was then the world's greatest military at Yorktown.

These sacrifices won our freedom. In 1791, Congress and the states ratified the Bill of Rights, including the First Amendment's prohibition on "abridging the freedom of speech." Never again would a government be able to invoke an "emergency" to censor the speech of the people. Never again would the American people have to endure the kind of review process for speech that still occurs in the United Kingdom to this day. Here the right to speak freely was of paramount importance.

As Justice Louis Brandeis said, our country's founders believed "that it is hazardous to discourage thought, hope and imagination; that fear breeds repression; that repression breeds hate; that hate menaces stable government; that the path of safety lies in the opportunity to discuss freely supposed grievances and proposed remedies; and that the fitting remedy for evil counsels is good ones." In other words, even if you *do* believe that the ideas someone is spreading are harmful, banning those ideas is not the solution. Even in the best-case scenario, you'll only make people *more* interested in the things you're banning, especially if those things later turn out to be true.

And worse, you'll end up fomenting serious mistrust of the government among the people.

The First Amendment has always been important to me. It had also been a topic in various commencement addresses I'd given. In 2018, I addressed my alma mater Saint Louis University's law school graduation class and noted,

> *In a recent poll, it was discovered that nearly forty percent of American adults can't name any rights listed in the First Amendment. A different poll showed that a growing plurality of Americans believe that the First Amendment goes too far because someone might be offended by something that someone else says. . . . Understanding what the First Amendment means and what it protects is fundamental. The First Amendment protects fundamental human expression, our freedom to speak our mind, worship as we choose, gather for a cause, write about what we see, petition our elected representatives for change. In short, the First Amendment is the beating heart of our Constitution.*

My entire address to the graduating class of the University of Missouri–Kansas City School of Law in 2019 was dedicated to protecting free speech, specifically on college campuses. It also played a starring role in a class I had taught at Saint Louis University. To me, the First Amendment is the beating heart of the Constitution and is central to our grand experiment of self-government.

This history was on my mind during the first months of Joe Biden's time in office, as the White House constantly censored the speech of Americans because it contradicted what public officials such as Dr. Anthony Fauci were saying. Just like the repressive British colonial government, the Biden Administration was policing the free speech of American citizens because it happened to go against the view of government officials. To them it was inconsistent with the regime narrative; that made it dangerous and therefore dissent must be crushed. Rather than doing it overtly, they appeared to be doing it in secret.

All we needed to do was prove it.

*

In the beginning, the information was all public ... well, sort of.

There, hiding in plain sight, was enough evidence to suggest that the Biden Administration had worked with social media companies to censor Americans. In my view, we'd all seen the tip of this censorship iceberg with social media companies gone wild back in October 2020, when a band of leftists at Twitter locked the *New York Post* out of its account for publishing an accurate story on Hunter Biden's salacious laptop (and stopped all users from even discussing the story using Twitter's direct message feature). We'd seen it when top scientists who disagreed with the Experts™ were banned from social media without being told why, often at the same time that they were being denounced by the White House.

Specifically, we had noticed the pressure that had been coming at social media companies from high-level Democrats, especially Joe Biden. During the 2020 campaign, in an interview with the *New York Times* editorial board, Biden had suggested that Mark Zuckerberg should face civil liability and even imprisonment for allowing Republican speech on his platforms—which sounded like a not-so-veiled threat: "He should be submitted to civil liability and his company to civil liability. . . . Whether he engaged in something and amounted to collusion that in fact caused harm that would in fact be equal to a criminal offense, that's a different issue. That's possible. That's possible—it could happen."

Moreover, Biden had taken an interest in Section 230 of the

Telecommunications Act, which gives broad protections to social media companies for the content that is published on their platforms. In short, the law says that social media companies, unlike newspapers and magazines (and even the *websites* for newspapers and magazines), are platforms rather than publishers. That might not sound like an important distinction, but it is. According to the law, publications like CNN and *The New York Times* are accountable for what they publish. That means they can be sued for content that is false. CNN and ABC News have recently settled eight- and nine-figure lawsuits on this front, though neither admitted to wrongdoing.

Twitter and Facebook, on the other hand, have long been viewed as *platforms*. In the eyes of the law, they are simply neutral arbiters that do not moderate content in any meaningful way. Because this shields them from liability for the content of speech on their platforms, it has been described as "a hidden subsidy worth billions of dollars" to tech platforms. But if you are Joe Biden and Kamala Harris or the Covidians sheltered in the West Wing, you want them to moderate, and maybe, just maybe they will if you tell them to or threaten them.

So, when Biden began telling people in late 2020 he wanted to revoke Section 230, while berating the social media companies for not doing enough to stop "misinformation," social media companies got the message. Again, speaking with what a reporter at *The New York Times* (hilariously) called his "late style," Biden said, "The idea that [Facebook] is a tech company is that Section 230 should be revoked, immediately should be revoked, number one. For Zuckerberg and all other platforms. And it should be revoked. It should be revoked because it is not merely an internet company. It is propagating falsehoods that they know to be false. . . . There is no editorial impact at all on Facebook. None. None whatsoever. It's irresponsible. It's totally irresponsible." This statement, and others like it, directly linked the threat of repealing Section 230—which is worth billions of dollars to the tech platforms—with Biden's demand that they censor speech that he dislikes.

Then Biden entered the White House, and the pressure on social media companies such as Facebook—which Biden, apparently under the inaccurate belief that Facebook posts had swayed the election for Donald Trump in 2016, had always singled out for special scorn—increased dramatically. This was ironic because no one had done more than Mark Zuckerberg to promote Biden's election, through the hundreds of millions of dollars of "Zuckerbucks" that he poured into Democratic voting areas. Shortly after he took office, Biden announced new actions to prevent "hate-motivated violence" that called for fundamental reforms to Section 230.

During Biden's first few months in office, he ramped up his public threats to social media companies, presumably because Democrats were now in charge of the Administrative State and were finding their sea legs in weaponizing Covid restrictions and expanding the role of government in our lives, thereby lessening our personal freedoms. This game was about punishing those who thought differently, and they had more levers of power now. They now had the immense power of the federal government, backed by Democratic control of both houses of Congress.

The introduction of vaccines brought things to a whole other level. On multiple occasions, Biden publicly accused these platforms—which occasionally allowed people to speak their minds about the dangers that vaccines might pose—of "killing people." Speaking from the White House in July 2021, he said, "They're killing people. The only pandemic we have is among the unvaccinated. And they're killing people." Later that year, Biden repeated the accusation, saying, "Look, the unvaccinated are responsible for their own choices. But those choices have been fueled by dangerous misinformation on cable TV and social media. You know, these companies and personalities are making money by peddling lies and allowing misinformation that can kill their own customers and their own supporters. It's wrong, it's immoral, and I call on the purveyors of these lies and misinformation to stop it. Stop it now." Thus Biden accused them of "killing people" *by not censoring the Covid-related speech* that Biden didn't like.

Even coming from a confused, shaky-voiced Joe Biden—who, even in his best days, was never a model of clarity—the message to social media companies could not have been clearer.

Do what we say, or we're coming for you.

Joe Biden's press secretary, Jen Psaki, even said the quiet part out loud: "We are in regular touch with the social media platforms and those engagements typically happen through members of our senior staff and also members of our Covid-19 team—given as Dr. [Vivek] Murthy conveyed, this is a big issue, of misinformation, specifically on the pandemic," Psaki said. She continued: "We've increased disinformation research and tracking within the Surgeon General's Office. We are flagging problematic posts for Facebook that spread disinformation." There it was. "Flagging problematic posts for Facebook." The Biden team was not even trying to hide that it was trying to censor speech online.

Knowing what I knew about the way government operates, of course, I knew there was probably much more going on under the surface. There was no way that the Biden-Harris Administration had simply made public threats, turned the cameras off, and called it a day. There must have been pressure from the highest levels of the Administration, and that pressure must have been applied behind closed doors. I knew from experience that there were only a few ways to blow those doors open. The first was through undercover journalism, some of which had been done already by excellent outlets such as *The Daily Wire* and *The Wall Street Journal*, as well as Mollie Hemingway of *The Federalist*. But there was only so much a reporter could do.

They could, for instance, connect the dots between posts that were being removed and the utterances of Dr. Anthony Fauci. During the heat of the Covid pandemic, I saw several of these reports and noticed a strange pattern. Whenever Dr. Fauci gave guidance, social media companies would begin banning anyone who disagreed with that guidance. This happened even when the people being banned were also doctors or researchers with advanced degrees (not that it should have mattered). These stories made valuable contributions to the public's understanding of just what the Biden-Harris Administration was up to.

But they weren't enough. In the end, there is only so much that a couple of investigative journalists can do while working against the federal government, especially now that the corporate press has effectively become the public relations arm of the Democrat Party. In another era, organizations such as the American Civil Liberties Union might have stepped in. For most of its history, the ACLU protected the freedom of speech even when it was deeply unpopular on the Left. It wasn't too long ago, for instance, that lawyers from the organization famously stepped up to defend neo-Nazis who wanted to march in a town of Holocaust survivors. They did this not because they agreed with the disgusting worldview of the neo-Nazis, but because they understood the most fundamental truth about free speech: that it means nothing unless you're willing to defend constitutionally protected speech that you find dangerous and abhorrent.

In recent years, though, as left-wing ideologues have taken over the organization, even the ACLU has become nothing more than an activist organization for Democrat causes. Rather than standing up against book bans, lawyers at the organization are tweeting that they will "die on the hill" of banning Abigail Shrier's book Irreversible Damage, which details the horrible consequences of sex-change surgeries in minors. Rather than standing up for those whose speech they oppose, they are shouting down speakers at colleges with slogans such as "The Constitution will not survive the Revolution."

In 2018, I participated in a forum on free speech with Nadine Strossen, the author of *HATE: Why We Should Resist It with Free Speech, Not Censorship*. She was the former longtime head of the ACLU and now lamented the ACLU's sellout.

As the strange saga of censorship continued to unfold, my team and I realized that there was probably only one way to shine light on what was going on, and that was a good, old-fashioned, Show Me State lawsuit. If the ACLU wasn't going to fulfill the mission that they'd set out for themselves at the turn of the twentieth century (namely to stand up for the rights of Americans no matter their political affiliations or philosophical inclinations), the Missouri Attorney General's Office would be more than happy to step in.

But I wanted a partner.

*

"Aw, I *love* that," said Jeff Landry in his distinctly Louisiana Cajun accent.

I had called Jeff one afternoon in the spring of 2022, thinking I would talk to him for a while and try to convince him to sign on to the lawsuit we'd been preparing against the Biden-Harris Administration over the censorship enterprise. I had mentioned it to his solicitor general, Liz Murrill, who is now the AG in Louisiana, at a recent RAGA meeting since Jeff wasn't there, but I knew Jeff would have final sign-off. I remember thinking that my chances were good. Like me, Jeff was an aggressive Attorney General. He'd brought several cases that drew attention to key hot-button issues of the day. His recent lawsuit involving offshore oil and gas leases had been particularly impressive. Not to mention that we also had a personal relationship. Just a few months before I called him, I had killed a decent-sized alligator at his annual gator hunt in the Louisiana bayou. That gator's hide would later be made into boots for me with the Missouri state seal on them just in time for me to be sworn in as America's two thousandth Senator.

In the end, I didn't have to do much convincing. Almost as soon as I finished my initial pitch for the lawsuit, Jeff was on board.

"I'm in," he said.

And we were off.

I hung up the phone and got to work, thinking of exactly the right way to bring the case.

On May 5, 2022, Missouri and Louisiana filed suit against the Biden Administration. The complaint included all of the evidence we had compiled covering more than two years, and it was written in a plain, accessible style that made the stakes clear. The first page of the complaint cited none other than President George Washington. In 1783, during an address to his army officers, Washington had said that if "the freedom of speech may be taken away," then "dumb and silent we may be led, like sheep, to the slaughter." In the same paragraph, it noted that "freedom of speech in the United States now faces one of its greatest assaults by federal government officials in the nation's history."

From there we laid out exactly what we believed the Biden Administration had been up to, marshaling all publicly available evidence to make the strongest case possible. It worked. In July 2022, the federal district court granted the request by Missouri and Louisiana to expedite preliminary-injunction-related discovery. We needed the discovery, the details, to make the case and we were now going to get it. Our gamble had paid off. The order allowed Missouri and Louisiana to conduct discovery and take depositions. In the weeks to come, we pored over documents that included emails, text messages, and official government memos that had never before been made public. We learned quickly that censorship in the Biden White

House was not a rare occurrence. Requests to take down accounts or stifle speech were as common as incomplete sentences by "the Big Guy" in the Oval Office.

In later filings with the court, the public would see for the first time, and could read for themselves, the extent of the censorship enterprise.

The official censorship efforts began just three days after the inauguration, when a White House official emailed Twitter to demand the removal of a tweet from Robert F. Kennedy Jr. The tweet in question mentioned the death of baseball legend Hank Aaron a couple of weeks after he received a Covid shot. Just days later, another White House staffer emailed Twitter asking for a tweet to come down because it contradicted something that Dr. Fauci and the Centers for Disease Control and Prevention (CDC) had said a few weeks earlier. The clear examples of censorship were so voluminous that the legal associates in my office often had to stay late into the night just to document them all. Below are just a few requests that the Biden White House made to social media companies.

- "Please remove this account immediately."
- "Cannot stress the degree to which this needs to be resolved immediately."
- "You are hiding the ball."
- "We are gravely concerned that your service is one of the top drivers of vaccine hesitancy—period. I will also be the first to acknowledge that borderline content offers no easy solutions. But we want to know that you're trying, we want to know how we can help, and we want to know that you're not playing a shell game with us when we ask you what is going on. This would all be a lot easier if you would just be straight with us."
- "[L]ooking out for your game plan on tackling vaccine hesitancy spread on your platform."

- "And while the product safari has been interesting, at the end of the day, I care mostly about what actions and changes you're making to ensure you're not making our country's vaccine hesitancy problem worse."
- "To recap: . . . we remain concerned that YouTube is 'funneling' people into hesitance and intensifying people's hesitancy. . . . [W]e want to be sure that you have a handle on vaccine hesitancy generally and are working toward making the problem better. This is a concern that is shared at the highest (and I mean highest) levels of the WH, so we'd like to continue a good-faith dialogue about what is going on under the hood here."
- "Would you mind looking at this video and helping us with next steps to put a label or remove it?"
- "Are you guys f**king serious? I want an answer on what happened here and I want it today."

Even if you didn't study constitutional law, you can probably tell that this is not the way anyone in the executive branch of our government should be speaking to private companies in the United States about the free speech of American citizens. These requests, backed up by threats of investigations and the revocation of Section 230, were a blatant violation of the First Amendment. Anyone who disagrees need only consult the Supreme Court's decision in *Biden v. Knight First Amendment Institute at Columbia University*. In that decision, the Court ruled that a private entity violates the First Amendment "if the government coerces or induces it to take action the government itself would not be permitted to do, such as censor expression of a lawful viewpoint. . . . The government cannot accomplish through threats of adverse government action what the Constitution prohibits it from doing directly."[2]

Reading through these messages, I was reminded of Oceania, the dystopian world that George Orwell created in his novel *1984*, which, ironically, I had reread, or in this instance listened to by way of audiobook, earlier in the year while painting some built-in shelves in our living room. Although politicians on both sides of the aisle often invoke Orwell (especially his best-known novel) to attack their enemies, I didn't see a way to avoid it in this case. Just before we filed *Missouri v. Biden*, the Administration had attempted to create a "Disinformation Governance Board" within the Department of Homeland Security. I assume they chose this because the name "Ministry of Truth" had already been taken by Orwell for his fictional dystopia. Either way, the effect would be the same. A panel of government experts would examine information and decide whether it was fit for public consumption—a chilling idea for anyone who cares about the freedom of speech.

In the end, the Biden Administration scrapped its plans to create a Ministry of Truth because of all the blowback. It helped that the censor-in-chief that they chose to run the board was Nina Janko-wicz, who had created cringe-worthy TikTok videos singing about censorship of conservative speech to tune of "Supercalifragilisticex-pialidocious" from *Mary Poppins*. But truth be told, the effort just went further underground. And it didn't stop several Democratic officials from attempting to censor information that might make Joe Biden and other Democrats look bad before much of the larger effort came to light. I'm sure we all recall being confused in October 2020 when the *New York Post* published its now-infamous bombshell story about salacious details found on the laptop of Hunter Biden. Back when we first filed *Missouri v. Biden*, very little was known about exactly what had gone on at the headquarters of Twitter during those crucial days and nights. All we knew was that somehow, a tech company prevented the American people from accessing crucial information about a presidential candidate in the lead-up to an election.

As part of our discovery in *Missouri v. Biden*, my team was able to take the deposition of Elvis Chan, the FBI agent who had helped to "pre-bunk" the Hunter Biden laptop story. For anyone who doesn't know how a "pre-bunk" operation works, allow me to explain. In November 2019 the FBI knew the Hunter Biden laptop was real. Yet they were telling social media companies to be on the lookout for a Russian "hack and leak" operation. What might that be? Well, Yoel Roth, Twitter's former head of "integrity and safety," told everyone in an affidavit filed with the Federal Elections Commission that he was told that the "hack and leak" operation would be about Hunter Biden. So, in advance of the 2020 election, the FBI "prebunked" the story they knew was real.

We blew this wide open and whistleblowers have since come forward to Representative Jim Jordan's committee in Congress. The FBI knew all of it. Why did they lie about it? What's on the laptop, and why were they working to help Biden unseat President Trump? All great questions we don't yet know the exact answers to, but then again, I think we actually do. What we do know for sure is this sequence of events and "pre-bunking" killed a story that most certainly would have had an impact on the 2020 election. What if Americans could have decided for themselves what all the photographs of Hunter Biden smoking crack nude with prostitutes, the records of his shady financial transactions, and all the angry texts to his family about money, should mean for their votes. And what was Joe Biden's role in all the foreign transactions?

Ultimately, the FBI decided to brief social media companies about a coming "dump" of "Russian propaganda" about Hunter Biden. Supervisory Agent Elvis Chan, a cybersecurity expert, was present at these meetings and testified about them.

This was never true, of course. The laptop was real, and so were all the incriminating materials on it—as the FBI had known since late 2019, when they *had the laptop in their possession*. But the FBI couldn't afford to have it spread. If it did, Joe Biden might lose the election of 2020, and Donald Trump might win again. Anything, in their view, was worth preventing that from happening. So, they lied. During our deposition of Chan, we learned that they lied *a lot*. And they were more than happy to tell the same lie repeatedly. For years, the American people had watched as the FBI, the Department of Justice, and the intelligence community led the liberal media on a wild goose chase to find evidence that Donald Trump had "colluded" with the Russians—something that then-Representative Adam Schiff said he'd seen evidence of in private, always in the hushed tones of someone who knew something top secret that would all be revealed soon. It turned out to be nonsense. But that didn't stop the FBI from pushing the lie to anyone who would listen. Anytime they heard something that might be harmful to Democrats, they labeled it "Russian disinformation." This allowed them to help ban speech without actually banning it.

As part of the preparation for my office's deposition of Elvis Chan, our office pored over files for days. His deposition made for an astonishing, eye-opening day. Chan was surprisingly open and forthright about the FBI's deep involvement in social media censorship—probably because he was extremely proud of his role in it, and he believed that there is simply nothing wrong with the most powerful federal law enforcement agency on earth dictating to Twitter, Facebook, or YouTube what Americans can and cannot post. Chan's admissions were so astonishing that on breaks during the deposition, our team of attorneys kept saying, "I can't believe he just said that!" Here are just a few highlights.

First and foremost, Chan basically admitted that the FBI had tricked and deceived social media platforms into censoring the *New York Post*'s Hunter Biden laptop story on October 14, 2020—an act of censorship so egregious that it could very well have swayed the outcome of the 2020 presidential election. Chan admitted that the FBI had endless meetings with platforms, including monthly group meetings and regular bilateral meetings, when the FBI encouraged platforms to censor political speech. During these meetings, Chan admitted, the FBI told platforms to expect a foreign "hack-and-leak" operation near the 2020 election, and the FBI encouraged platforms to adopt policies requiring them to censor "hacked" materials—which the platforms did. As Twitter executive Yoel Roth would later admit, federal officials even warned the platforms that the supposed "hack-and-leak" operation *would involve Hunter Biden*. During this time, the FBI had Hunter Biden's laptop in its possession since 2019 and *knew* that the laptop was not "hacked" materials. Then, when the story broke, the FBI refused to confirm that the laptop was not "hacked" when the platforms immediately inquired. As a result, Twitter and Facebook treated the laptop's contents as "hack-and-leak" materials and censored them—just as the FBI had *deliberately led them to believe even though the FBI knew it was not true*. Facebook aggressively suppressed the story, which would later be told in great detail by Miranda Devine at the *New York Post*, in news feeds, and Twitter was even worse—it suspended the *New York Post*'s Twitter account for two weeks, thus silencing the oldest daily newspaper in the United States! As Chan revealed (and Mark Zuckerberg and Twitter later admitted), federal law enforcement officials, and not the platforms, were responsible for one of the most momentous, egregious acts of social-media censorship in American history.

There were many other highlights of the Chan deposition. For example, Chan revealed that, ever since 2017 (after President Trump was first elected), the FBI had brokered secret meetings in Silicon Valley between high-level congressional staffers and the platforms to talk about censorship. The congressional staffers evidently pressured the social media companies into greater censorship by showing them potential adverse legislation in the meetings. Chan argued that the FBI only targeted "foreign" disinformation, but in fact the reality was very different. The FBI would find simple posts that supposedly originated from foreign sources communicating common political messages like "Support the Second Amendment!" or "Secure the Border!" or even "Down with Hillary!" The FBI would then push the platforms like Facebook, Twitter, and YouTube to censor these posts. But the FBI would do so only after thousands or hundreds of thousands of Americans had "liked," re-posted, or commented on them. So, while claiming to censor "foreign" speech, the FBI was also censoring the core political speech of hundreds of thousands of Americans.

Other depositions were equally eye-opening. Senior federal officials were deeply embedded with social media platforms, pressuring and collaborating with them to censor ordinary Americans' speech. In fact, some federal agencies had entire divisions dedicated to censorship. The deposition of Brian Scully of the Cybersecurity & Infrastructure Security Agency was a jaw-dropping example. CISA is an unknown alphabet-soup subdivision of the Department of Homeland Security. But instead of protecting us from cyberattacks, which is its real job, CISA goes all-in on protecting us from "misinformation" and "disinformation"—which is another word for "opinions that the government does not like." As Scully admitted, CISA orchestrated the creation of the so-called Election Integrity Partnership, an immensely sophisticated operation run by researchers at Stanford University and other elite institutions. Closely cooperating with CISA and dozens of other government officials, these "researchers" obtained privileged access to the platforms and had dozens and dozens of snoops "flagging" so-called "misinformation" to platforms during the 2020 election cycle. This resulted in literally tens of millions of posts being censored—all core political speech of ordinary Americans. And they got away with it completely. In fact, it worked so well that, as soon as the 2020 election was over and Biden was in office, they restarted the same game to censor Covid-related "misinformation," silencing the voices of millions of Americans on social media, all done in close collaboration with federal government officials. Your tax dollars hard at work, silencing you from describing your experience with Covid vaccines or sharing your candid thoughts about election integrity in America!

Things were equally bad at the Centers for Disease Control and Prevention, part of the Department of Health and Human Services. The deposition of the CDC witness, Carol Crawford, revealed that, due to Biden Administration pressure, Facebook and other platforms had basically outsourced their decision-making about what to censor to CDC officials. During the Covid pandemic, Facebook's senior content moderation officer, Liz Lagone, would simply email the CDC with long lists of statements that people were making about Covid on Facebook—including many claims that later turned out to be absolutely true. Thus Facebook would just ask the CDC, please tell us what to censor! And the CDC would happily oblige, going claim-by-claim through the list and telling Facebook what it should and should not allow people to say on their Facebook pages. This process got even worse when big, controversial announcements came—such as the approval of Covid vaccines for children, and later for young children and infants. Then Facebook would email the CDC *beforehand* and ask them to say *in advance* what should be censored when the announcement came out. This is what constitutional law calls a "prior restraint" on speech—the very worst kind of First Amendment violation.

Worst of all was the Biden White House itself. Through dogged persistence in litigation, and multiple emergency appeals by the federal government, our litigation team obtained the emails between social media platforms and White House Director of Digital Communications Rob Flaherty—a name that should live in infamy in the annals of the First Amendment. These emails were an astonishing treasure trove of information. They revealed that the Biden White House had, from its first days in office, aggressively pressured, threatened, and coerced the platforms like Facebook, Twitter, and YouTube to censor speech that they did not like. On Biden's third day in office, a Biden White House official emailed Twitter and demanded that it take down a post by Robert F. Kennedy Jr., demanding that Twitter "get moving on the process for having it removed ASAP." Flaherty and senior White House official Andy Slavitt ran a two-prong pressure campaign against the platforms for the next several months. They badgered platforms for information about their censorship policies and continuously demanded ever-greater censorship of speech they did not like. They demanded the censorship of high-profile speakers and critics of the Biden Administration like Tucker Carlson, RFK Jr., Alex Berenson, and many others. They specifically pressured Twitter to deplatform Berenson—and succeeded. They repeatedly demanded the censorship of content that *did not violate the platforms' community standards.* They were particularly focused on censoring what they called "often-true" speech, which the White House opposed *because it was true,* and thus was *effective* in publicly criticizing the White House's Covid tyranny.

They demanded immediate action in removing Twitter accounts, saying things like "Please remove this account immediately," and "Cannot stress the degree to which this needs to be resolved immediately." They repeatedly demanded that Facebook "partner" with the White House on censorship. When they did not get the answers they wanted, they made ominous, threatening statements to platforms like "this comes from the highest (and I mean highest) levels of the WH," "You are hiding the ball," "the last time we did this dance, it ended in an insurrection," and "Internally we are considering our options on what to do about it." When all that didn't work, they lashed out at the platforms in profane language. Once, when Flaherty did not get the answer he wanted right away on one question about censorship, he wrote to Facebook, "Are you guys f**king serious? I want an answer on what happened here and I want it today.""* (Flaherty did not use asterisks in his email—he used the full F-word—but this is a family-friendly book.)

This private pressure campaign was reinforced by public statements from the White House. White House Press Secretary Jen Psaki publicly admitted that "we're flagging problematic posts for Facebook." She and White House Communications Director Kate Bedingfield made public statements linking the White House's demands for greater censorship to threats of a "robust anti-trust program," threats to hold platforms "accountable" and "legally liable" for Americans' speech, and threats to repeal the liability protections of Section 230 of the Communications Decency Act. To Silicon Valley insiders, threatening federal antitrust enforcement and repeal of Section 230 are "existential" threats for the platforms, designed to go for the jugular and bend the platforms to the White House's will.

And it worked. This monthslong pressure campaign came to a head in July 2021 when Biden publicly stated about the platforms, "They're killing people" by not censoring enough Covid-related speech. After this, the platforms buckled under and did whatever the federal government demanded. They promptly deplatformed Alex Berenson and a long list of disfavored speakers. They quietly adopted aggressive new censorship policies to target the speech that the federal government didn't like. They scrambled to get back into the White House's good graces, begging officials to tell them "what the White House expects of us on misinformation going forward"—so that they could censor whatever the White House

---

*The platform's answer was highly ironic. Flaherty and the White House were furious that Facebook had apparently flatlined President Biden's Instagram followers. After Flaherty cussed them out, Facebook officials privately admitted that their algorithm had been accidentally treating Biden's account as a possible purveyor of Covid "misinformation" and censoring it. In other words, Facebook had accidentally imposed the very same censorship rules *that the White House had demanded for ordinary Americans* on the White House itself. Needless to say, the hypocrites in charge at the White House were *absolutely furious* when they found that they had been victim to the same rules they'd forced Facebook to apply to everyone else.

wanted them to. As noted above, they started sending lists of statements to the CDC to ask the CDC what to censor. Facebook's head of global affairs, former UK Deputy Prime Minister Nick Clegg, told the White House, "we hear your call for us to do more" in censoring Americans' speech—and they answered that call.

What is perhaps most astonishing is that this is just the tip of the iceberg. In discovery, my team asked Twitter to identify all the federal officials in the Biden Administration who communicated with Twitter about censoring speech. In August 2022, Twitter identified eleven people—a number that my team thought was impossibly low. But then, in November 2022, Twitter was acquired by Elon Musk. Two months later, Twitter "revised" its disclosure and revealed that at least *eighty-three* federal officials were doing so—including at least *twenty* White House officials. Of those twenty, we only obtained emails and documents from *one*—Rob Flaherty. There are *nineteen* more whose emails, to this day, we have never read. But even the White House's sophisticated, coordinated, and very successful censorship campaign paled in comparison to the crown prince of censorship, Dr. Anthony Fauci.

*

Dr. Fauci walked into the conference room at the National Institutes for Health (NIH) in Maryland ten minutes or so after the rest of us had gathered. The place had more security than nearly any place I'd been, save the White House. We all shook hands, then sat down. Dr. Fauci and four or so Justice Department lawyers sat to his left. John Sauer, who would lead the questioning, sat directly across from Dr. Fauci, I was immediately to his right, and Jeff Landry was to my right. Another dozen or so individuals, including staff and some named plaintiffs, were allowed in the room and sat on chairs up against the wall in the forty-by-seventy-foot room.

Our team had carefully prepared for the deposition of Dr. Fauci. We knew he would be a tough witness. He routinely made media appearances and testified before Congress. He was smart, disciplined, and experienced. But he also appeared to be extremely arrogant. He had made statements like "If you criticize me, you are criticizing Science™." And this, we expected, would make him vulnerable to patient, relentless, disciplined questioning.

Even though the questioning lasted seven hours, there was barely enough time to cover all Dr. Fauci's activities. We wanted to cover several main themes in the deposition. All of them revealed a common theme that I summarized on a Twitter post afterward: When Dr. Fauci talks, social media censors.

First, and most important, we wanted to address Dr. Fauci's insidious attempt to induce the platforms to censor the lab-leak theory—the idea that Covid did not come from naturally from bats, but it was a deadly, bioengineered virus that leaked from the Wuhan Institute of Virology. This part of the deposition took half a day, with much resistance and obfuscation by Dr. Fauci, but it revealed that Dr. Fauci's own National Institute of Allergy and Infectious Diseases had funded dangerous virus-enhancing research at the Wuhan Institute of Virology and thus their credibility would be badly damaged if a dangerous, enhanced virus had escaped from that lab and touched off a global pandemic.

To avoid this prospect, Dr. Fauci secretly conspired with other science-funding authorities and orchestrated a scientific paper discrediting the lab-leak theory, and then he cleverly fed that paper to compliant reporters at a White House press conference—directly undermining President Trump in the process—as if it were an independent study. The media followed Dr. Fauci's lead, dismissing the lab-leak theory as a racist, xenophobic conspiracy theory. Social media platforms followed suit and censored the theory. For the better part of two years, it was unspeakable on Facebook or Twitter to say that Covid might have leaked from a lab—until government agencies started admitting that, far from a conspiracy theory, it was probably true.

In addition, we drilled Dr. Fauci on his collaboration with Dr. Francis Collins to censor the leading critics of the "lockdown" approach to Covid—an approach that Dr. Fauci and his staff effectively borrowed from Communist China at the beginning of the pandemic. In October 2020, prominent scientists from Harvard, Stanford, and Oxford organized the "Great Barrington Declaration," criticizing the harsh lockdown approach to Covid. Due to their enormous bravery, these scientists presented a grave threat to the totalitarian response to Covid endorsed by Dr. Fauci and his allies. Once the declaration was published, Dr. Collins emailed Dr. Fauci demanding a "quick and devastating published take-down" of this criticism of the government's totalitarian policies. Dr. Fauci obliged, pushing his personal opinions out to the media as scientific facts, claiming that the Barrington Declaration was "fringe," "nonsense," and "very dangerous." Again, social media immediately followed suit, suppressing the Barrington Declaration. (Ironically one of these men became a plaintiff in *Missouri v. Biden*, a friend and now NIH director Dr. Jay Bhattacharya.)

Dr. Fauci's treatment of masks, moreover, contrasted starkly with his treatment of alternative Covid treatments like ivermectin and hydroxychloroquine. Though he endorsed mandatory masking without any scientific evidence, he demanded full-blown, double-blind, randomized clinical trials demonstrating effectiveness before anyone could try such alternatives. Such scientific certainty never existed for masks, of course.

Dr. Fauci's deposition revealed the enormous power of a single federal official to effectively control what millions of Americans could and could not say on social media about some of the most important, hotly disputed questions of the day. Early in his deposition,

Dr. Fauci was caught in a series of inconsistencies where he would testify one way, and then get confronted with a document that contradicted him. So, in a classic Washington, D.C., pirouette, he pivoted to claiming that he could not recall. By the end, he had said "I do not recall" 174 times, and variations of "I do not remember" at least 212 times. These included claims that he "could not recall" details that, not long before, he had told reporters, "I remember it very well." Despite this obfuscation, Dr. Fauci could not hide the truth—he had personally orchestrated the censorship of millions of Americans on social media.

Things began pleasantly enough. John asked questions. Dr. Fauci gave basic answers, none of which contained any information we couldn't have gotten on Wikipedia. As the deposition went on, though, a clearer picture emerged of exactly how Fauci operated. For the first time, he was made to answer for the email he sent to a colleague in February 2020 saying that masks were ineffective, something he confirmed on March 31.

The lab-leak theory, which Dr. Fauci had worked overtime to discredit along with his allies in the mainstream media, also came up. As Dr. Fauci waffled and said, "I don't recall," his true motivations emerged. On the table were documents in which Dr. Fauci had acknowledged that the lab-leak theory had merit. All the while, he maintained publicly that the theory was nonsense, and that Covid-19 could not have leaked from a lab. He maintained this, of course, because he knew that a lab leak could be traced directly back to him and his team at the National Institutes of Health.

There were other bright spots. Through careful questioning, John was able to get Dr. Fauci to admit on the record (sort of) that he had sent his deputy, Dr. Clifford Lane, to China during the early days of the pandemic to see how the Chinese Communist Party was responding to the disease. From a series of documents and Dr. Fauci's reactions to them, it became abundantly clear that Fauci and Lane had designed the lockdown strategy to which the people of the United States were later subjected after the Chinese Communist model. They also appeared to take cues from the CCP when it came to censoring anything the government didn't like.

At one point during the deposition, the court reporter sneezed. Dr. Fauci asked her tersely to put on a mask, and she complied. From there it was "I don't recall," and "I'm not sure," and "I don't remember." In the end, Dr. Fauci dodged many questions by claiming he could not recall anything about the most damning documents. But sometimes, getting someone on the record is good enough. Immediately after the deposition, we knew we had laid a foundation that others could build on. Although it took a while, we did manage to release the deposition in full, and it is still available online today. Reading it, you get a full portrait of an Expert™ being called to account for the first time. You see someone who thought he could lie for years, dispensing advice that contradicted the best scientific advice to stroke his ego, and not get caught. In my opinion, Dr. Fauci didn't think he would get caught because he had the devoted protection of the legacy media. He thought the pandemic gave him cover, and he didn't believe that anyone would have the guts to dig through his record and find out what he got up to during those crucial first months of the pandemic.

I'm happy to say he was wrong about that.

*

Eventually, *Missouri v. Biden* (by then styled *Murthy v. Missouri*) went to the Supreme Court.

In earlier proceedings, the U.S. District Court for the Western District of Louisiana issued an injunction blocking federal officials from influencing content moderation. The Fifth Circuit Court of Appeals later upheld most of this injunction but limited its scope, specifically preventing government officials from actions that could coerce social media platforms to restrict protected speech. However, in October 2023, the Supreme Court granted the Biden Administration's request to lift the injunction while it considered the case, allowing the government to continue engaging with social media companies without restrictions. In *Murthy v. Missouri*, the Supreme Court later dissolved the injunction on the ground that the plaintiffs had supposedly not provided enough evidence of "standing," or the level of injury required to sue. While I disagree with that decision, I note that as of the publication of this book, the case is still proceeding on the merits in the Western District of Louisiana, and the federal judges who considered the *merits* of our claims—the trial judge, the three appellate judges in the Fifth Circuit, and three Supreme Court justices in a separate opinion in *Murthy*—held that the Biden Administration was egregiously violating the First Amendment by pressuring, coercing, and harassing social media platforms to silence disfavored viewpoints, especially criticism of the government and its policies. As the district court put it in its opinion, "the present case arguably involves the most massive attack against free speech in United States' history."

There has been plenty of other evidence. We were all shocked (in a good way) when Elon Musk finally purchased Twitter in 2022 and then promptly aired the company's very dirty laundry for all to see. There, written in black-and-white digital ink, was corroboration of everything we had been looking for—and finding—during the discovery phase of *Missouri v. Biden*. We finally saw records of the emails between the Biden-Harris Administration and the censors at Twitter. We learned what happened on the morning of January 7, when a bunch of Big Tech employees decided that they had the right to censor the President of the United States for speech they had deemed unfavorable.

As mentioned in the introduction, Mark Zuckerberg himself

admitted that he faced unwelcome pressure from the Biden-Harris Administration to censor truthful information about Covid-19, including humor and satire. Reading his letter, I felt vindicated in a way that I've been getting used to lately—and even more so when he announced that Facebook would abandon its aggressive censorship policies. Clearly, the information we uncovered during the discovery phase of *Missouri v. Biden* was information that the people of the United States—and the world—needed to hear. We had won the argument.

And thank God—the future of our Republic depends on it.

Part III

Protecting American Sovereignty

Chapter 8

MISSOURI, TEXAS V. BIDEN: HOLDING BACK THE FLOOD

There's no arguing that immigration is a national issue. In fact, it might be *the* defining national issue, given that a nation simply cannot exist without borders. When anyone can just come into America without any screening or following our legal process and get the benefits that come with citizenship—things like the right to vote, welfare, and housing—the term *American citizen* becomes meaningless. Immigration isn't just about who comes in; it's about ensuring that those who do are willing to embrace the values and principles that define the nation. A country has the right—not just the right, but the obligation—to select for people who respect its laws, culture, and way of life. Without that, national identity erodes, and the foundation of the republic weakens.

President Trump understood this from the moment he stepped onto the national stage (or, more accurately, when he rode down the golden escalator into the Trump Tower lobby to announce his candidacy). Much to the chagrin of the legacy media at the time, the future president laid out the problems with our immigration system in clear, plain language that brought the issue to the forefront of our national conversation. During his four years in the White House, he worked hard to fix our broken immigration system. Beyond beginning construction of his famous border wall, there were plenty of behind-the-scenes efforts that made our southern border safer than it had ever been before.

One of the most important policies was called "Remain in Mexico." Negotiated with President Andrés Manuel López Obrador near the end of President Trump's time in office, the policy stated simply that anyone wanting to apply for asylum in the United States needed to wait in Mexico while their claims were processed. It was a solution to a serious problem. In previous administrations, hundreds of thousands of people had come into the United States, claimed asylum, and then disappeared before they could have their claims processed. When it came time for these people to show up in court, they were nowhere to be found.

Sometimes these stories ended in tragedy. In 2015, for instance, a young woman named Kate Steinle was killed when an illegal immigrant with multiple previous deportations and felony convictions dropped his gun, discharging a bullet that struck her. The same thing happened to Mollie Tibbetts, a college student in Iowa, who was murdered by Cristhian Bahena Rivera, an undocumented farmworker. Unlike previous occupants of the Oval Office, President Trump met with the families of these young women and vowed to take action. Simply allowing hundreds of thousands of people to pour into the country while they awaited the processing of their (often bogus) claims of asylum wasn't something he could tolerate.

The Remain in Mexico policy did not stop people from South and Central America from claiming asylum. It only said that they needed to wait in Mexico while their claims were processed. Thus it deterred the bogus asylum-seekers (the ones who would make a phony claim and then disappear into the United States) from coming in the first place, and it stopped the cartels from facilitating mass migration. The policy was a resounding success. Right away, we saw a sharp reduction in the rate of illegal immigration, which hit a then–record low of 36,000 crossings per month in 2019. The flood of illegal migrants pouring into the United States slowed down enough to give the men and women of our Border Patrol some much-needed relief. The policy sent about 65,000 people who were in the United States waiting for claims to be processed back to Mexico, where they were housed by the Mexican government. In just a few months, President Trump had done something that was (and still is) rare in Washington, D.C. He had implemented a policy that did exactly what he said it was going to do, and he'd improved the lives of American citizens while doing it and America had its most secure border in forty-five years.

Then came Joe Biden.

*

Throughout the 2020 campaign season, as Democrats struggled to distinguish themselves in a crowd of dozens of would-be candidates, immigration came up often. By this point, with the implementation of pandemic restrictions such as Title 42, illegal immigration had hit levels that many people didn't believe was possible. By the time President Trump was wrapping up his time in office, we had seen a 53 percent reduction in the number of encounters at the border. For once, a president had come into office and accomplished something he said he'd get done—a serious reduction in illegal immigration—even in the face of enormous obstruction from the other side of the aisle.

The Democrats didn't like that. For years, they had been telling us that any opposition to immigration of any kind—even opposition to *illegal* immigration—was racist. It hadn't always been that way. As recently as the 1990s, the platform of the Democratic Party had included strong language about the need to keep our borders secure. In 1996, when Bill Clinton was running for his second term in office, the official platform read:

> *We must remain a nation of laws. We cannot tolerate illegal immigration, and we must stop it. For years . . . Washington talked*

tough but failed to act.... Our borders might as well not have
existed. The border was under-patrolled, and what patrols there
were, were under-equipped. Drugs flowed freely. Illegal immigration
was rampant. Criminal immigrants, deported after committing
crimes in America, returned the very next day to commit crimes
again.

As the writer Matt Welch put it in *Reason* magazine, the document has "reverse-resonance" in today's Democratic Party, no member of which would be caught dead using such language about immigration in public.

And it wasn't just the 1990s. Back when Barack Obama was a newly elected Senator from Illinois, Democrats supported the Secure Fence Act of 2006, which authorized the construction of 700 miles of physical barriers along the U.S.–Mexico border. Obama, along with other prominent Democrats, including then–Senators Hillary Clinton and Chuck Schumer, voted in favor of this bill. The act was part of a bipartisan effort to enhance border security by building fencing and implementing additional surveillance technologies.

It's clear when things changed. The Democratic Party's shift on immigration coincided with its abandonment of the blue-collar workers who had once been its backbone. By the time Barack Obama left office, it was virtually forbidden for anyone in the party to suggest that illegal immigration might be a problem. Somehow, the same people who would soon be demanding that Americans show vaccine passports just to enter a TGI Friday's had no problem letting millions of people stream into the United States without so much as signing a piece of paper. Between the early 2000s and 2020, illegal immigration became the single most serious issue facing our nation. As Barack Obama's two terms in office wore on, it became almost impossible for Democrats to speak clearly or tell the truth about the need to keep our borders secure. Their focus had shifted away from working-class Americans and toward a new coalition—one in which enforcing immigration laws was seen as an obstacle rather than a necessity.

It wasn't until President Trump took office in 2017 that we began to make serious strides on this issue. He increased deportations of illegal immigrants, particularly focusing on those with criminal records, and prioritized immigration enforcement within the interior of the country. He also expanded the use of ICE detainers to ensure that local law enforcement cooperated with federal immigration authorities, which helped reduce the number of illegal immigrants who were able to avoid deportation after being arrested. Furthermore, the administration ramped up workplace raids targeting employers who hired undocumented workers, a move that aimed to reduce the incentive for illegal immigration by cutting down on job opportunities for those entering the country unlawfully.

And the American people responded positively to all of it.

So, if they were going to beat him, Democrats needed to run from the opposite direction. (You see this now in President Trump's second term as well.) From the moment Joe Biden and Kamala Harris hit the campaign trail in 2020, they both promised to undo the crucial protections that the Trump Administration had put in place. Kamala, in particular, used her eleven minutes of fame to hit the Trump Administration hard on immigration. During an appearance on *The View*, she said, "Let me be very clear: We have to have a secure border. But I am in favor of saying that we're not going to treat people who are undocumented [and] cross the borders as criminals. . . . What we cannot do is have any more policy like we have under this current president that is about inhumane conduct."[1]

Biden was worse. During the first Democratic primary debate in June 2019, he said, "What I would do as president is several more things. I would in fact make sure that there is . . . we immediately surge to the border, all those people who are seeking asylum."[2]

As the campaign ramped up, Biden singled out the Remain in Mexico policy for particular scorn. In March 2020, obviously trying to court the votes of the woke Left so he'd win the nomination, he tweeted, Donald Trump's "Remain in Mexico" policy is dangerous, inhumane, and goes against everything we stand for as a nation of immigrants. My administration will end it.[3] As the campaign wore on, the promises piled up. Biden and Harris would turn the nation into an open-borders hellscape to please their far-left interest groups, and there was nothing anyone could do about it.

Once he got into office, Joe Biden and Kamala Harris took the same woke scattershot approach to immigration that they'd taken to everything else. Whatever President Trump had done, they did the opposite. They raised taxes on the middle class because President Trump had lowered them. They created the conditions for new foreign conflicts to arise, the opposite of what President Trump had done. And they opened up the border because President Trump had effectively closed it—and, of course, because they had promised many far-left affinity groups that they would do so.

Luckily, you can't just open the American border by signing a piece of paper. If *that* were possible, you can bet that Biden would have done it on day one. What you *really* have to do is take a series of smaller steps, every one of which erodes our southern border a little more. You have to end Title 42, for instance, and stop construction on the border wall. You have to send a message to the world that the door to the United States is officially open, and that anyone who shows up will get in.

Still, a president can do quite a lot of damage with a few strokes of a pen, which is exactly what Biden did during his first days in office. Sitting in the White House in January 2021, President Biden suspended the deportation of illegal aliens for one hundred days. He also stopped illegal immigrants from being enrolled in the Remain in Mexico program, the official name of which was the Migrant

Protection Protocols policy. At that very moment, according to the ultraliberal news outlet NPR, "Thousands more migrants from Latin America [had] pushed their way toward Mexico. . . . Some [had] told journalists that they [were] making their way north because they expect it to be easier to enter the U.S. under the Biden Administration."[4]

Which, as you might expect, was a mild way to put it.

At the same time Joe Biden was signing his ninety-plus executive orders undoing all the successful Trump initiatives, massive caravans of migrants were making their way north. They had been paying attention during the campaign of 2020, knowing that if Biden and Harris managed to win, the doors to the United States would be open. And unlike President Trump, Biden wasn't going to make them wait it out in Mexico while their claims were being processed. Bogus asylum-seekers by thousands, or even millions, would be allowed simply to arrive at the southern border, claim asylum, and then disappear into the United States. The flood was coming, fueled by American taxpayer dollars to NGOs no less, and there seemed to be nothing anyone could do to stop it.

At least that's how it felt in the days immediately following Joe Biden's inauguration. Remember that for those first few weeks, we had seen clear evidence that the system was hell-bent on working against the conservative movement in the United States (as if we needed more of that). Big Tech and the Democrats had colluded—yes, *colluded*—to sway the election for Joe Biden, and now Joe and his far-left cronies were working to remake the United States of America in their own open-borders image. It was easy to feel dejected and despondent, especially when you were paying attention to the news.

But when it came down to it, the Remain in Mexico program was a regulation with the force of law. It had been challenged in the courts before, and it had come out relatively unscathed. After reviewing the actual texts of the executive order as well as the original Remain in Mexico policy documents, my team and I became convinced that the best way to fight Biden was to take him to court. There, politics shouldn't matter. All that mattered was the law, specifically whether Biden had the authority to end a program that had been so successful in keeping Americans safe.

Once again, I didn't think we should do it alone.

So, I called up the one person I knew who was as fired up about fighting Biden's border policies as I was: Attorney General Ken Paxton of Texas.

*

Now, if you're smart enough to have made it this far in a book about the American legal system, I probably don't need to tell you that Texas is a border state and Missouri is not. But when you think about it, that's kind of the point.

Under the leadership of Joe Biden and his Border Czar Kamala Harris, *every state* became a border state. When those illegal migrants streamed over the border into the United States, signed their papers, and then went free, they really *went free*. No one was keeping track of them. That meant they ended up in New York City; La Crosse, Wisconsin; Seattle, Washington; and yes, *Missouri*. During the first weeks of the Biden Administration, my office had gotten reports of many illegal migrants congregating in places all over our state. In many cases, we would learn that Joe Biden and the federal government had helped get them there. According to a report from the Center for Immigration Studies, Biden spent $86 million on bus rides and chartered flights to get migrants from the southern border to cities all over the nation, none of whom were equipped to deal with the sudden influx of so many people. Moreover, as a powerful expert affidavit that we filed would explain, Biden's open-borders policies made Missouri a particular hub for human trafficking due to its place at the heartland of America in the intersection of major interstate highways. Biden's open borders led directly to a spike in human trafficking in Missouri, including coerced sex-trafficking of minors and children. Fentanyl came pouring across our borders like never before as well.

With that in mind, I figured that a lawsuit coming from two states—one of which had been dealing with the immigration issue for decades, and another one that would soon be dealing with it just as seriously thanks to Joe Biden—was the best way of getting our message across. So we began drafting a complaint and worked with the Texas Attorney General's Office. We wanted our lawsuit to be *the* suit that kept the Migrant Protection Protocols in place. Even now, I believe it stands as a master class in finding state grounding for federal issues.

"In the first several hours following President Biden's inauguration," we wrote,

> *the incoming administration discontinued implementing the successful Migrant Protection Protocols (MPP). These regulations required individuals who both lacked a legal basis to be present in the United States and who had passed through Mexico en route to the United States to remain in Mexico pending adjudication of their immigration claims. Prior to the MPP, individuals passing through Mexico could enter the United States, raise asylum claims, expect to be released into the United States in violation of statutory requirements mandating their detention, and stay in the U.S. for years pending the resolution of their claims—even though most were ultimately rejected in court. MPP changed the incentives for economic migrants with weak asylum claims, and therefore reduced the flow of aliens—including aliens who are victims of human trafficking—to the southern border.*
>
> *This lawsuit challenges the Administration's unexplained and inexplicable two-sentence statement suspending the MPP, as well as*

its latest memorandum permanently terminating MPP. The result of these arbitrary and capricious actions has been a huge surge of Central American migrants, including thousands of unaccompanied minors, passing through Mexico in order to advance meritless asylum claims at the U.S. border.

This migrant surge has inflicted serious costs on Texas as organized crime and drug cartels prey on migrant communities and children through human trafficking, violence, extortion, sexual assault, and exploitation. These crimes directly affect Texas and its border communities, especially given Texas's strong focus on combating human trafficking both at the border and throughout the State. The additional costs of housing, educating, and providing healthcare and other social services for trafficking victims or illegal aliens further burden Texas and its taxpayers.

The effects of unlawful immigration do not stop at the southern border. Indeed, "[t]he pervasiveness of federal regulation does not diminish the importance of immigration policy to the States," which "bear many of the consequences of unlawful immigration." . . . With its intersection of major interstate highway routes, Missouri is a major destination and hub for human trafficking. Missouri's ongoing fight against human trafficking—including the exploitation and trafficking of vulnerable migrants—likewise provides it with justiciable interests that fall within the zone of interests of federal statutes on immigration-related policy. Indeed, irresponsible border-security policies that invite and encourage human traffickers to exploit vulnerable border-crossing victims irreparably injure Missouri and other States.

With the broad facts and the stakes of the case outlined, we moved on to the actual violations of law that Joe Biden's Department of Homeland Security had committed when attempting to repeal Remain in Mexico. As usual, these violations centered on how Biden's DHS had ignored standard procedures by abruptly ending the policy without a clear explanation, which broke federal rules about how policy changes need to be carefully reviewed and justified, and how they failed to uphold existing immigration laws that require certain migrants to be detained while their cases are being reviewed.

We filed this lawsuit on April 13, 2021, in the Northern District of Texas, and the initial hearings began shortly thereafter. One crucial goal for us was to have the judge grant an injunction that would reinstate the Remain in Mexico policy while the case was being litigated, including on appeal.

Which, on August 13, 2021, is exactly what happened. Judge Matthew Kacsmaryk ruled in our favor, issuing a permanent injunction ordering the Biden Administration to resume the Remain in Mexico program while the case worked its way through the appellate courts. And despite several attempts to stay the injunction, the Biden-Harris DHS was forced to comply. In August 2021, the U.S. Supreme Court denied the Biden Administration's application to stay the injunction, requiring them to obey the injunction and to continue implementing Remain in Mexico for months to come. The Supreme Court specifically noted that we were likely to prevail on our claim that the cancellation of the Remain in Mexico policy violated the Administrative Procedure Act (APA).

This initial win was also important in setting the stage for the public debate that would follow. That fall, tens of thousands of migrants were prevented from entering into the United States, where they might have disappeared for good while they waited for their claims to be processed. It wasn't a perfect fix for the problem, especially given that the number of migrants streaming into the United States was still skyrocketing, but it did manage to hold back the flood for a time. During the monthslong period when the Biden-Harris DHS was forced to put the Migrant Protection Protocols back in place, more than 73,000 illegal immigrants were sent back to Mexico for processing; another 5,000 were prevented from entering the country at all.

Predictably, the Left went insane, claiming that deporting migrants back to Mexico would expose them to dangerous conditions. Writing in a brief to the Supreme Court, the ACLU—which, it seems, only springs into action lately on behalf of left-wing causes rather than violations of the rights of American citizens—wrote that the program had "put asylum seekers directly in harm's way," and that "asylum seekers returned to Mexico are sent to some of the most violent areas in the world."[5] Democratic lawmakers adhered to the same party line.

What they ignored, however, was that an open invitation to enter the U.S. would drive even more people into the hands of smugglers and traffickers. Studies show that over 60 percent of migrants are subjected to violence or exploitation during their journey, with many passing through cartel-controlled areas in Mexico. Human-trafficking profits in this region are estimated at $13 billion annually, fed by a steady flow of migrants seeking asylum. Curbing this cycle requires reducing the number of people risking the journey—not increasing it. And lowering the standards for entry would only increase the journey, thus subjecting far too many people to unnecessary suffering.

Once the Supreme Court held that the Biden Administration likely violated the APA by terminating the program, the Administration tried multiple do-overs, including reassessing the entire issue and issuing a new memorandum (twice) to supposedly justify canceling the program. Unfortunately, when the Supreme Court finally decided the case in June 2022, five out of the nine justices agreed that Joe Biden did, in fact, have the authority to end the program, based on the second do-over. Following its end, millions of migrants who would have otherwise been detained were allowed into the interior of the United States. Of course, it is important to keep in mind that these encounters with Border Patrol are simply the ones we know about. There were almost certainly many more who managed to evade capture.

All throughout the campaign of 2024, Republicans recognized that illegal immigration was a growing crisis. Democrats, on the other hand, continued to pretend it didn't matter. Their refusal to acknowledge the problem became a political liability, and their unpopular stance was a major factor in the landslide reelection of President Trump in 2024.

For conservatives, this wasn't just about winning elections—it was about ensuring that the rule of law still meant something.

As we saw during President Trump's first term in office (and now during his second term), sometimes the right answers to our immigration problems are the simplest ones. When you enforce our immigration laws, fewer people will come illegally. When you make people wait in Mexico while their immigration claims are processed rather than allowing them to roam free in the United States before their court dates, fewer people will raise bogus claims of asylum. The problem with the Left in this country has never been that they don't know what works. Most of them know full well how to stop people from getting into this country illegally.

The problem with the Left, as well as those in the corporate media who cover for them, is that they don't *want* our immigration system to work. They want more illegal aliens to come in because they think it means more people who will be voting Democrat. They want to change the makeup of this country because they believe that Latino people—or, as white liberals call them, "members of the Latinx community"—will reliably vote for left-wing policies. (Of course, as we saw in 2020 and again in 2024, this is not even remotely true.) That is why, when it comes to the sovereignty of our nation and the security of our borders, we are long past the point at which we can negotiate with the Left. Sometimes the only option is taking them to court and racking up whatever wins we can get.

Which brings me to one of the simplest methods for securing our border: a good, old-fashioned wall.

Chapter 9

MISSOURI, TEXAS V. BIDEN
PART II: BUILD THE DAMN WALL

Walls work.

If you don't believe me, try getting from one room to another without using the door.

But in the Trump era, when liberals have allowed their hatred of one man to cloud their judgment and critical thinking skills completely, even simple facts such as this one are up for debate. Suddenly, liberals are no longer sure that when Joe Biden decided to throw open our Southern Border, that might have had something to do with the massive spike in illegal immigration. They no longer admit, as they did in 2006, that having a physical barrier along our southern border is the best and most practical way to keep people from treating it like the front door of a 1990s Best Buy on Black Friday.

We've already seen how quickly Joe Biden attempted to undo the Trump Administration's Migrant Protection Protocols. Although we weren't able to fully stop him from repealing those protocols, we managed to hold back the flood for several months, saving a great deal of money (and American lives) in the process. What we haven't yet discussed is how hard the Biden Administration went after a signature achievement of President Trump.

The Wall.

For years, there has been no better way to make a liberal's head explode than to tell them we need to finish building the border wall. Something about it seems to offend them on a visceral level. In part, the reason we keep hearing about it is that it remains the simplest and most effective way to secure our border.

In some places, it has already happened.

In the Yuma Sector of Arizona, for instance, illegal entries dropped by 87 percent after new border wall sections were completed. Similarly, in the Rio Grande Valley, apprehensions fell by 79 percent after the completion of a wall system in that area. These areas are some of the most heavily trafficked for illegal crossings, and the border wall helped direct the flow of migration toward ports of entry, where enforcement was stronger. Additionally, in the San Diego Sector, CBP saw substantial efficiency improvements, with the wall reducing manpower needs by 150 agents every twenty-four hours, allowing for more targeted border security efforts.

According to the latest estimates, a complete wall would reduce traffic at the border by about 80 percent in high-traffic areas. It would stop the flow of people, potentially saving millions of women and children from falling victim to human trafficking at the hands of the drug cartels. As soon as it gets built and all that happens, liberals will have no choice but to admit that President Trump had a point.

Perhaps that is why they attempted to stop him at every step of the way while he was in the White House. Every time another steel beam went up along the roughly two thousand miles of land that separate Texas, New Mexico, Arizona, and California from Mexico, we would get another press release from the left-wing congressional Squad about how building walls is equivalent to fascism. I'm sure we all remember seeing Representative Alexandria Ocasio-Cortez showing up at the border wall in all-white, posing for the camera in tears as she stared out into Mexico.

Of course, these people have no problems putting up walls to protect their own gated communities. They were more than happy to put a massive fence around the Capitol Building after January 6, 2021. But when it comes to the entrance of our nation, the same rules didn't apply. Down there, the Left has long preferred a complete free-for-all. This lack of willingness to even admit we have a problem has cost us many human lives over the years. It has also frustrated the men and women of our Border Patrol, who, before President Trump came into office, had come to feel that their needs weren't being met. As soon as President Biden hit the Oval Office, he moved immediately to divert the funds that the United States Congress had appropriated for the wall—about $1.375 billion in total. The problem for Biden was that this was plainly illegal. Congress had passed, and President Trump had signed, an appropriation *act* directing that this money be spent to build the border wall. That directive had the force of law, and Biden could not just ignore that law—but he did.

Working once again with Attorney General Ken Paxton of Texas, I devised a way to put the people of Missouri—the very ones I was elected to protect—at the center of the fight to secure our borders. The ongoing flow of illegal migrants into the United States wasn't just a border issue; it was affecting states like Missouri. Human trafficking, drug smuggling, and criminal networks fueled by this crisis didn't stop at the southern border—they made their way into the heart of the country, victimizing innocent Missourians.

The case was straightforward. Attorney General Paxton and I argued that the Biden Administration's decision to halt border wall construction violated the law. Congress had already set aside $1.375 billion for the wall in the Consolidated Appropriations Act of 2021, and just as much money in a similar act the year before. By refusing to use these funds, the Administration wasn't just shirking its duty; it was violating the Constitution's Take Care Clause, which requires the President to faithfully execute the laws passed by Congress. This failure to act left both Missouri and Texas vulnerable to the unchecked surge of illegal migrants and the criminal elements that prey on them.

This time, however, the initial ruling was not favorable. The

Southern District of Texas, which heard the case initially, ruled that we did not have standing to bring the lawsuit. According to the court's decision, our claim—that the Administration's refusal to build the border wall was directly harming Missouri—was deemed too indirect. The court stated that while border states like Texas might experience tangible effects from illegal immigration, Missouri was too far removed from the immediate impact of border issues to claim direct injury. The judge, an appointee of George W. Bush, argued that we hadn't sufficiently demonstrated how halting the wall's construction had harmed the people of Missouri.

There was another wrinkle. Around the same time, the Texas General Land Office (GLO) filed suit against the Biden Administration. Leading the charge was George P. Bush, the Texas land commissioner. Unlike our lawsuit, the GLO's case centered on specific harm that would come to state-leased land along the Texas–Mexico border. The office claimed that halting the border wall construction had turned that leased land into a "superhighway" for illegal border crossings, causing environmental and security issues.

In the opinion of the judge who reviewed our case for the Southern District of Texas, both suits could not proceed at the same time. This supposed conflict, known as "claim splitting," prevents different agencies within a state from suing on behalf of the state in some circumstances. For these two reasons, our lawsuit was thrown out. However, we appealed in the Fifth Circuit, where a three-judge panel overturned the ruling of the judge in the Southern District of Texas and ruled in our favor. Writing for the majority on June 16, 2023, two of these judges said, "The district court abused its discretion in dismissing Texas on the ground that it improperly split its claims." It also dismissed the standing issue, sending us back to the Southern District of Texas.

And just like that, we were back in business.

*

Reading through the stories in this book so far, you might wonder why things go so differently in different courts. After all, our argument didn't change between the initial hearing and the appeal. The facts on the ground didn't change either. There was *still* over $2 billion waiting to be spent on the border wall, and Joe Biden was *still* trying to stop it from being used for that purpose. The objections of Missouri and Texas were the same.

The answer, sadly, lies with judges.

All over the country, federal judges are given broad discretion in interpreting the law. This is a complicated task, and there are many different ways of going about it. In general, we on the conservative right tend to believe that the laws, as written, mean what they mean, not what we *want* them to mean. We believe that the Constitution has a fixed meaning that doesn't change with the times.

Legal scholars and judges on the Left have, historically, taken a different approach—one that we saw play out in terrifying ways in previous chapters. But it's not only the Supreme Court. At the federal level, left-wing judges can still do a great deal of harm. They can interpret the Constitution to contain a panoply of unwritten "rights" (always favorable to the Left) and interpret statutes to mean the opposite of what they plainly were written to mean. Unfortunately, it is up to presidents to nominate these judges, and Democrat presidents did a much better job than conservative ones of nominating judges throughout the twentieth century. During the twelve years that President Franklin Delano Roosevelt was in office, for instance, he nominated 193 federal judges and three Supreme Court justices. Before him, President Woodrow Wilson—a man who is probably responsible for more bad policy than any single human being in the history of the United States—managed to nominate 75 federal judges.

It wasn't until the early 1980s that the conservative movement began to catch up. By then, the future of American law was liberal and bleak. Law schools, especially those in the Ivy League, had drifted so far to the left that conservative students had begun to feel like embattled, beleaguered outsiders. As we saw in a previous chapter, the Supreme Court had just handed down a string of decisions that made a mockery of the Constitution. Under the leadership of Chief Justice Earl Warren, they had created new rights that were never in the Constitution in the first place, including the nonexistent "right to privacy" that served as the foundation for the court's infamous decision in *Roe v. Wade* (one that even the ultra-liberal Ruth Bader Ginsburg admitted was probably built on shaky ground). Now, at Harvard Law School and other elite institutions, a left-wing movement known as critical legal studies was gaining steam.

As the liberal writer Jeffrey Toobin has written, this strange movement "was a hybrid of traditional Marxism and contemporary literary theory; its adherents purported to expose the contradictions and class biases inherent in all aspects of law. . . . They portrayed law as first and foremost an instrument of oppression of the disenfranchised, and they did so in a manner that was both passionate and obscure, with articles full of citations to the work of 'poststructuralists' like Jacques Derrida. Crits and conservatives on the faculty battled over tenure appointments, and the fights sometimes spilled into the classrooms, and even into courtrooms. The Kremlin on the Charles became known as Beirut on the Charles."[1]

Against this backdrop of infighting and confusion, a group of students at Yale and the University of Chicago Law School got together and formed a small group that was meant to stand for conservative legal principles. At the University of Chicago, the faculty advisor to the first few students was none other than future Supreme Court Justice Antonin Scalia. At Yale it was Robert Bork, another luminary in the conservative movement (whose nomination to the Supreme Court would, unfortunately, soon be derailed by the Left). From the beginning, the Federalist Society—named for the people who ratified the Constitution of the United States—advocated a return to the basics. Rather than creating new rights where none existed, they maintained that the Constitution said what it said, nothing more and nothing less.

Over the course of the next forty years, law students who came up through the Federalist Society found themselves with many key appointments around the country. The group created a deep bench of like-minded jurists who could take the country back from the more permissive, left-wing ideologues who had come to control our federal court system.

President Ronald Reagan nominated many conservatives to the federal bench, and so did Presidents George W. Bush and George H. W. Bush. But their efforts have paled in comparison to those of President Donald Trump, who identified the American judiciary early on in his first term as one of his best opportunities to leave his mark on this country. For one thing, judicial appointments in the twentieth century tended to be based more on personal relationships than anything else. Someone went to law school with someone, or a Senator had a good friend from back home who wanted the job. It wasn't necessarily seen as a way to remake the government. But President Trump saw things differently. From the moment he entered the Oval Office, he was on the lookout for talent. Working with Leonard Leo, the head of the Federalist Society, and Senate Republicans, President Trump adhered to a system for vetting judicial nominations that was amazing to watch. Every time he put another name forward, I would cheer from the sidelines, knowing that my chances of being tossed out of court by some liberal, Trump-hating judge just went down a few percentage points.

Like so much else in the Trump 45 White House, the work on

judicial nominations never stopped. And that work in Trump 47 is already underway. His work ethic and stamina are legendary. By the end of his first term, President Trump had managed to nominate more than 230 federal judges, all of whom adhered to good conservative principles. At the time the only president ever to have nominated more was George Washington (although that's only because Washington didn't have any to start with).

One of those judges, as it turned out, was a Texas-born corporate lawyer and former U.S. marine named Drew Tipton. Tipton had attended a state college and a state university, where he'd been a member of the Federalist Society. From there he'd worked in the private sector before being tapped by Donald Trump to serve on the District Court for the Southern District of Texas in 2020. He was confirmed by a vote of 52–41 in February of that year, and he began his work on the bench shortly thereafter. One of his first cases, as it turned out, was *Missouri, Texas v. Biden*, which came right back to him after the Fifth Circuit sent the case back to the Southern District of Texas on appeal. And unlike the Bush-appointed judge who had dismissed us for claim splitting and lack of standing the first time around, Judge Tipton looked at the case on its merits and ruled accordingly.

A few months after he received the case, he granted a preliminary injunction against the Biden Administration, emphasizing that the executive branch did not have the authority to unilaterally divert funds that Congress had *explicitly* allocated for the construction of the border wall. Judge Tipton's ruling focused on the constitutional principle that the executive branch must adhere to the laws passed by Congress, particularly regarding the appropriation of funds. He pointed out that the law was clear: The funds were designated for the border barrier, and the Administration could not bypass this directive.

As Judge Tipton's order effectively pointed out, this was not the case where Congress had passed a broad statute giving the executive branch some latitude or discretion on how to spend the money. That practice is regrettably common, and is the sort of latitude or discretion that, we know now, the Biden Administration was then abusing through agencies like the Agency for International Development, or USAID, and the Environmental Protection Agency to expend appropriated funds unlawfully by steering money to their pet left-wing causes and to their political allies—"Throwing gold bars off the *Titanic*," as on Biden staffer said. That is how they were funding projects like publishing transgender comic books in Peru, sex-change operations in Guatemala, and billion-dollar giveaways to leftist political agitators like Stacey Abrams. In this case, instead of unlawfully abusing its authority to expend money on unlawful causes, the Biden Administration was unlawfully abusing its authority by *not* spending the money the Congress (and President Trump) had commanded it to spend on one very specific purpose specified in the statute: "construction of a barrier system along the southwest border." As Judge Tipton's order reveals, the Biden Administration acted unlawfully in both instances.

Tipton's ruling effectively blocked the Biden Administration from repurposing the $2.75 billion that Congress had approved for the border wall under the Consolidated Appropriations Act. Thanks to our lawsuit, and our willingness to stick with the case (and, in large part, to President Trump's steadfast dedication to returning this country to constitutional principles), our state lawsuit managed to have a serious effect on the federal appropriations process. The ruling, which came down in March 2024, came just in time for President Trump to make his triumphant return to office. In this case, just like so many others, all the conservative legal community needed to do was fight back for long enough to stop the

Biden Administration from undoing one of President Trump's signature policies, and we needed to do it for as long as it took for him to get back to office. In that we succeeded, which is why we may yet see a "big, beautiful wall" get finished at some point over the next couple of years.

Chapter 10

FIGHTING FOR TITLE 42

During the early months of Covid-19, it was *Democrats* who had begun telling us that we couldn't simply allow people to go out in public without documentation or express permission from the government. It was Democrats who were now more afraid than ever of strange people entering their communities and potentially spreading a disease that we knew very little about at the time. For a few seconds, I assumed that we might be able to reach some common ground on the most pressing national issue of our time.

But it didn't happen. Almost immediately after President Trump began suggesting that he would use the pandemic as justification for further border security measures, the Left reacted with the same outrage as they had in the aftermath of his decision to shut down all flights from China—a decision that, as we've seen, probably saved millions of lives. Even Dr. Fauci himself called it "a very prudent decision."

Luckily, the "national emergency" that the Left would soon use to trample on the rights of Americans also gave the President an opportunity. Working with members of his administration, President Trump invoked a series of protocols from the mid-twentieth century called Title 42. Officially, these laws were known as the Public Health Service Act of 1944, and they covered public health measures, including quarantine and the prevention of communicable diseases. But it was the section granting the CDC director authority to prevent the entry of persons during a public health crisis that President Trump was most interested in.

On March 20, 2020, he announced that Title 42 would be invoked to swiftly expel migrants at the U.S.–Mexico border in order to prevent the spread of Covid-19. This emergency measure allowed border officials to bypass normal immigration protocols and quickly deport individuals without all the red tape that they were forced to endure in normal circumstances. In a sense, this was a move designed to tie left-wing brains into pretzels. Either they could say that it was a racist an unnecessary move, thereby conceding that Covid-19 was not a major crisis, or they could support it, tacitly admitting that borders work. Either way, liberals had no choice but to live with it. As long as the "national emergency" designation of Covid-19 lasted, so too would the provisions of Title 42.

This, as you might imagine, led to some of the lowest illegal immigration figures in our nation's history. Immediately after the policy went into effect, we were seeing a record low of 16,000 encounters per month, a level that would have been unthinkable under any other administration. (For reference, Joe Biden's first full month in office saw just over 100,000 encounters, a number that continued to increase during his time in the White House.)

But it couldn't last. As soon as Joe Biden took office, we began hearing rumblings that Biden would soon end Title 42, presumably because of pressure from left-wing interest groups who believed that the United States should have a completely open border. But it didn't happen right away. For a full year after he took office, Joe and his Justice Department continued the Title 42 provisions, arguing in court that they were still necessary to prevent the spread of Covid-19 near the border. Speaking during a hearing on the matter in January 2022, a Justice Department attorney said, "Under the Title 42 order . . . non-citizens can be rapidly screened, and then quickly expelled, substantially reducing the risk of transmission."[1]

But the pressure from left-wing interest groups continued to mount. Briefs from the ACLU—which had by now strayed completely from its original mission—rolled in. An attorney for the organization called Title 42 a "brutal policy against families." For months, organizations like the ACLU had engaged in negotiations with the Biden Administration to make Title 42 less effective. As part of one court ruling, the government was prevented from expelling migrants who were traveling with children. Every day, we got closer to the moment when the far Left brought the bureaucrats of the Biden Administration around to their way of thinking on the subject—specifically, that Covid-19 was a major problem everywhere *but* the southern border, and that we should once again throw the gates open for anyone who wanted to come in. To these people, pandemic provisions such as widespread mail-in ballots and mask mandates would need to stick around forever. Title 42, on the other hand, the *only* provision that had been demonstrably effective at reducing the spread of the virus—as well as violence, drugs, and human trafficking—needed to go.

The moment came in March 2022. This time, President Biden didn't even announce the policy himself, likely because he (or whoever was *actually* managing the White House at the time) knew just how bad things were about to get. In a short announcement, a spokesperson for the CDC said, "After considering current public health conditions and an increased availability of tools to fight COVID-19 (such as highly effective vaccines and therapeutics), the CDC Director has determined that an Order suspending the right to introduce migrants into the United States is no longer necessary."

The provisions of Title 42, according to the announcement, would expire on May 23, 2022, just two months after the announcement.

Unless, of course, someone did something to stop it.

Which is where we came in.

*

From the beginning, it was clear that Title 42 probably wasn't going to last forever. The policy was based on the state of emergency surrounding Covid-19, and we knew that this probably couldn't be used as a permanent justification for keeping our borders closed. But when it came to the crisis that was unfolding every day at the southern border of this country, we were willing to try anything to help slow things down.

So we reached out to the office of Mark Brnovich, the Attorney General of Arizona, and learned that he and a few other states were planning to file a lawsuit imminently. The plan, as usual, was to get a preliminary injunction to buy some time and hold back the flood. To do so, we gathered evidence and looked around for all the people who had admitted that ending Title 42 would be a horrible idea. Many of them, as it turned out, were Democrats. Just a few weeks earlier, Senator Joe Manchin had said that revoking Title 42 would be a "frightening decision," explaining that the United States was "nowhere near prepared to deal with that influx. Until we have comprehensive, bipartisan immigration reform that commits to securing our borders and providing a pathway to citizenship for qualified immigrants, Title 42 must stay in place." He'd also said, "Title 42 has been an essential tool in combatting the spread of COVID-19 and controlling the influx of migration at our southern border. . . . We are already facing an unprecedented increase in migrants this year, and that will only get worse if the Administration ends the Title 42 policy."[2]

To some Democrats and liberal media figures, having the Senator from West Virginia weigh in on matters of illegal immigration was laughable. *Literally.* During coverage of the midterm elections in 2022, former White House communications director Jen Psaki would laugh with Rachel Maddow about voters from Virginia being concerned about illegal immigration, suggesting that the only thing they *really* had to fear was people from West Virginia coming over the border. But Senator Manchin, like many people living in land-locked states, was beginning to understand that immigration was no longer an issue that affected only people who lived within a few hundred miles of the border. It was now *everyone's* problem.

In our complaint, which was submitted to the Fifth Circuit on April 12, 2022, we included quotes from many other Democratic Senators, most of whom did not represent border states. We quoted Democrat Maggie Hassan of New Hampshire, who said, "Ending Title 42 prematurely will likely lead to a migrant surge that the administration does not appear to be ready for." We quoted Republican Bill Cassidy of Louisiana, who said, "Removing Title 42 is a mistake that will encourage another wave of illegal migration and drug trafficking to overwhelm the Sothern Border. There is no justification for this." To bolster the point, we found interviews with people from all across the political spectrum, focusing specifically on the Border Patrol agents who would have to bear the brunt of the coming invasion. One, speaking anonymously to Fox News, had said, "We're preparing to get wrecked."

It's important to note that this wasn't some fringe view. In the lead-up to the decision to end Title 42, even members of the Biden Administration were bracing for an enormous surge at the border. But the pressure from the Left had become too much to bear, and the decision was made. Luckily, a growing number of states were willing to join our lawsuit to stop this from happening. In our initial filing, three of those states—Arizona, Louisiana, and Missouri—outlined the specific harm that would befall our citizens if Title 42 were revoked. In our section, we pulled in all that data we'd been collecting on this issue since Joe Biden took office, including figures suggesting that approximately 56 out of every 1,000 illegal aliens who entered the United States at the time would eventually come to reside in

Missouri. We cited crime figures, pointing out that Missouri is a hub for many criminals due to the confluence of several major interstate highways within the state. Above all, of course, there was the increased cost that illegal immigrants would force the state to incur, as well as the jobs that would be lost for American citizens.

All of these elements were crucial to establish state standing in this federal case, which Missouri had become great at by this point in time. However, the real thrust of our argument rested on procedural violations of the Administrative Procedure Act (APA). We claimed that the Biden administration had failed to engage in the proper notice-and-comment rulemaking process, a requirement under the APA. By not providing sufficient public notice or an opportunity for stakeholders to comment before rescinding Title 42, the administration bypassed critical procedural safeguards meant to ensure transparency and accountability. As esoteric as all that might sound, it was exactly what we needed to say in court to get the injunction we were looking for.

On April 25, 2022, District Judge Robert R. Summerhays—who, it bears mentioning, was among the 234 federal judges nominated by President Trump—granted our request for a temporary injunction. For the time being, the Biden Administration was forced to keep Title 42 in place, momentarily holding back the huge influx of migrants. But there were obstacles. When you're fighting against the federal government, there always are.

A few months after we were granted our temporary injunction allowing Title 42 to remain in place, a different lawsuit signaled the end of the program. This one, which happened in Washington, D.C., was decided by Judge Emmet G. Sullivan, a man whose name had become notorious to Republicans due to his gross mishandling of several cases having to do with the Trump–Russia Hoax. One of these cases, which concerned charges against National Security Advisor Michael Flynn, went so poorly that Judge Neomi Rao of the

United States Court of Appeals for the District of Columbia Circuit called his actions "highly irregular," and said they reflected "an inexplicable insistence on prolonging the case."

He handled the Title 42 case about as well, ruling that the program would need to end in December 2022. Right away, our coalition attempted to intervene in the case.

However, the writing was on the wall. Given that Title 42 was, at its root, a public health measure, it would expire whenever the Biden Administration decided to lift its state of emergency for Covid-19. And despite the best efforts of those on the Left to prolong the crisis for political gain, that *was* going to happen eventually. On May 11, 2023, the state of emergency was lifted, and the provisions of Title 42 went with it.

The gates were open again.

*

Sadly, the results were predictable.

In the aftermath of Title 42, encounters with illegal migrants surged to the highest levels ever recorded. By May 2023, we had seen more than 200,000 people every month streaming into the United States. And it's important to point out, once again, that these were the people we knew about. Every day, an estimated 1,500 people escape the Border Patrol and get right into the country without anyone ever noticing that they exist.

On the Left, politicians and activists were outraged. But it wasn't the sudden influx of illegal migrants that got them upset. It was the fact that the rule the Biden Administration reverted to after Title 42 (which was called Title 8, a much softer version that did not allow for the swift deportation of migrants) was *still* too harsh for them. Speaking shortly after the largest surge in migration in modern American history, a Democratic member of Congress from Illinois said, "It's evidence that there's been an unmistakable shift in the president's immigration policy. I know the administration is in a tough spot, but it's beyond disappointing to see them trying to appease Republicans on immigration."

That was mild. A few months earlier, just after we'd filed our initial suit, an activist in Texas said, "Title 42 was never about public health, but rather is shrouded in racism, as doctors and public health experts have made clear that immigration is not a source of pandemic spread. Now, President Biden must keep his promise to undo Trump's anti-immigrant policies and take the only right and moral path forward: fight this decision and use every administrative tool at his disposal to fight back against the right-wing extremists who lead the states that brought the suit, including Louisiana and Arizona."[3]

Seeing quotes like this, I was annoyed. And it wasn't only because these people tended, for whatever reason, to leave out the great state of Missouri. It was because I could see that no matter how hard we might try to have a common understanding with fellow Americans, even on the Left on the issue of border security, the Left wasn't going to budge. Even though all we were asking the Democratic Party to do was nudge themselves slightly back toward the center— which, as we've seen, was exactly where they were as recently as the early 2000s—they continued to drift leftward. Anything less than a fully open border was not going to satisfy them.

In 2023, when I became a United States Senator, I saw many of these battles play out in a way I couldn't have imagined when I was still the Attorney General of Missouri. During this time, border crossings were still surging. And given that there was an election coming up, Joe Biden and the Democrats finally began to sense that they needed to do something—or at least pretend to do something—to address the issue. Without some action on immigration, the Democrats knew they were heading for a resounding loss on election day.

First, there were negotiations about a potential border bill. While Democrats claimed that the bill would solve the problem at the border just before the election, it did nothing of the sort. In reality, the proposed border bill was a disaster. It created an express lane for illegal immigration, weakened existing law, and made America less safe. It normalized the daily crossings of thousands of illegal immigrants and handed broad, unchecked authority to individuals and agencies already proven to be ineffective—or outright unwilling—to address the crisis. The so-called "shutdown authority" it gave to Secretary of Homeland Security Alejandro Mayorkas and President Biden was riddled with exceptions, sunsets, and loopholes, rendering it meaningless. Even worse, legal challenges to the bill were funneled through the D.C. District appeals court, bypassing judicial circuits that had traditionally handled border issues. This effectively ensured that any challenge to the Democrats' policies would be dead on arrival.

The bill also authorized nonjudicial officers to decide asylum claims, bypassing the immigration court system entirely and further opening the floodgates for unchecked migration. Perhaps most damning of all, one of the lead Democratic negotiators admitted publicly, "The border never closes under this bill." It was evident that this was never meant to be a real solution; it was a political stunt, a desperate attempt to stop the bleeding at the polls ahead of the election and disingenuously try to shift blame for the border crisis to Republicans. I had said over and over that we didn't need new laws, just a president who wanted to enforce the laws we have. I had litigated against the Biden Administration and saw their true colors on this issue. They had no desire to secure the border. It was a conscious choice and the results were disastrous. But they were making a long-term electoral play, since you don't need to be a citizen to be counted in the census and if you made the problem so big, that was their path to mass amnesty.

This bill we were to consider wasn't just poorly conceived—it was negotiated in secret and meant to be shoved through Congress with almost no time for meaningful debate or review. It was also meant to be a fig leaf for $60 billion in additional aid to Ukraine meant to—ironically—protect the sovereignty of their borders. Democrats expected Senators to vote on this massive spending package without the transparency and deliberation the American people deserve. It was another slap in the face to border states and to law-abiding citizens across the country. In the end, the bill fell apart under its own weight, but Ukraine later got their money anyway.

Meanwhile, the crisis worsened. By 2024, at least ten million illegal immigrants had crossed the border under Biden's watch, including 1.8 million known "gotaways" who evaded Border Patrol entirely. Fentanyl deaths were up by 94 percent since 2019, and at least eighty individuals on the terror watch list were caught trying to cross the border. The FBI warned that the porous border posed a major terror threat. Despite this, Democrats continued to block commonsense measures like the Laken Riley Act and H.R. 2, which would have deported illegal immigrants who assaulted police officers or allowed local law enforcement to detain migrants committing crimes.

But then, everything changed. The American people spoke loudly and decisively in the 2024 presidential election. Donald Trump was reelected, and with his return to the White House came a renewed commitment to restoring law and order at the border. For the first time in years, there was real hope for a solution.

Under President Trump's leadership, many of the policies that had worked before—especially strict enforcement of immigration laws—have been swiftly reinstated. The chaos at the border immediately began to subside. The days of Democrats playing political games with the safety and security of the American people were over. We were vindicated as well. We didn't need new laws, just a new president. As I reflect on these battles, I feel a deep sense of pride for the role Missouri played in standing up for border security and the rule of law. But I also feel a renewed determination. The fight to secure our borders and protect our nation is never truly over. And as long as I am in public service, it will remain my mission to ensure that the mistakes of the Biden Administration are never repeated. With Donald J. Trump back in office, we don't have to deal with the daily disasters created by the Left's open-border policies anymore. America is once again on a path toward safety, sovereignty, and strength.

Part IV

Dismantling the
Administrative State

Chapter 11

CHIPPING AWAY

O ver the course of this book, we've discussed many lawsuits that I brought on behalf of the people of Missouri. Some of them began in my home state. But many of them didn't. In some sense, my team and I were not unlike legal first responders running toward danger to help those in need. It didn't matter where the trouble was.

This was particularly true in the case of the Administrative State.

From the moment I took office, I knew that I wanted to chip away at the federal government's vast network of regulations. I wanted to use my office to take on the unelected bureaucrats who, for over one hundred years, had grabbed far too much power from the legislative branch with no accountability. Before he left office to become a Senator, my predecessor, Josh Hawley, had supported the Trump Administration as it made changes that would lead to the challenge that would make the biggest dent in the Administrative State that we'd seen in decades.

It was called *West Virginia v. EPA*, and the dispute dated back to the Obama Administration. To make a long story short—which is always necessary when you're dealing with cases involving the vast bureaucracy of the federal government—the whole thing began when the Obama Administration promoted a regulation known as the Clean Power Plan, which set national limits on carbon pollution from power plants and laid out a plan to shift states from coal to renewable energy sources such as wind and solar. Once again, the liberals had used the language of an urgent "emergency" to change rules (with the force and effect of law) without resorting to Congress, which is where laws are supposed to be made.

Among its many provisions, the Clean Power Plan said that "fossil fuel–fired power plants must significantly reduce their carbon dioxide emissions by shifting generation to cleaner energy sources, such as natural gas, wind, and solar."

Note that these words did not come from Congress, which is the branch that should, according to the Constitution, be issuing such proclamations. It came from the Environmental Protection Agency, one of the many organizations within the executive branch that has come to make most of the policy in the United States. Unlike the people in Congress and the White House, the people who work at the EPA aren't elected by anyone; most of them aren't even *appointed* by people who are elected. They go about their business without fear that they'll have to answer to the American people. This, in the opinion of many conservatives (this one included), is fundamentally at odds with the United States Constitution.

One of my other predecessors thought so too.

Chris Koster, a Republican turned Democrat running for governor, and his team at the Missouri AG's office had joined with West Virginia in a lawsuit against the EPA that challenged the organization's authority to enact such broad regulations. Working alongside companies like Murray Energy Corporation and Peabody Energy, West Virginia argued that it was Congress, not federal agencies, that should be making policies of this kind. In early 2016, the Supreme Court issued a stay in the case, meaning that the Clean Power Plan couldn't be enforced while the legal challenges were being decided. The case was set to go to court when, tragically, Justice Antonin Scalia passed away, leaving the court with an even eight members. Thanks to the clever procedural maneuvering of Senate Republicans, Barack Obama was not able to nominate a left-wing successor to Justice Scalia. Instead, President Trump took office, and one of his administration's first moves was to roll back the Clean Power Plan (which resulted in the dismissal of the cases challenging the Clean Power Plan because there was nothing left to challenge, or in legal terms, the case was moot). Under the leadership of Scott Pruitt, the EPA introduced something known as the Affordable Clean Energy Rule, which imposed far less stringent regulations for coal-fired power plants.

I happened to take office as Attorney General of Missouri shortly before the Affordable Clean Energy Rule was finalized, which occurred in June 2019. As I watched them from afar, I had a feeling that we hadn't seen the last of the case. It is important to note that while the Trump Administration did get rid of the underlying rule that caused the lawsuit, the legal controversy didn't just go away. Groups on the Left challenged the Affordable Clean Energy Rule, and I joined an effort led by Patrick Morrisey, then–Attorney General of West Virginia, to intervene in defense of the Trump Administration. Lawsuits continued to work their way through courts, every one of which hinged on obscure legal questions and matters of policy minutiae. As with most things in the Administrative State, the case was boring. That, in a sense, is kind of the point.

This is also why courts matter so much to conservatives. Normal people don't have the time to track every convoluted regulation that bureaucrats dream up, and they shouldn't have to. But the courts can. Judges and Attorneys General serve as a necessary check on unelected officials who use legal loopholes and bureaucratic red tape to push policies that would never survive a public vote. Without strong courts willing to uphold the Constitution, the Administrative State would run unchecked, slowly reshaping the country in ways most Americans never agreed to.

But the underlying question was the same. Did a giant group of unelected bureaucrats have the right to effectively make laws that would affect the lives of the American people? As the AG of Missouri, representing more than six million of those American citizens, I didn't think so. In part, that was because the people of Missouri did have a genuine stake in the outcome of *West Virginia v. EPA*. As we said in the initial brief, the EPA's overreach threatened to "increase electricity prices for Missouri families and businesses" and "undermine the reliability of the state's energy grid, which relies heavily on coal-fired power plants."

However, I also knew that the case was part of a much larger legal fight—one that would affect the lives of Americans in far more serious ways in the years to come if we didn't do something about it. Just like some of the other fights my team and I took on from the Missouri Supreme Court building, it was a fight between the forces of tyranny and freedom. Liberals were on one side, and we were on the other. But unlike our fights against mask mandates, Big Tech censorship, and woke schooling, this one had been going on for a *long* time. It concerned the very structure of our government.

And it began, oddly enough, with the father of the modern Administrative State, President Woodrow Wilson.

*

From the moment he was born in 1856, Woodrow Wilson loved nothing more than telling other people what to do. He was, as I like to put it, the "OG progressive." According to a biography of him written by A. Scott Berg, Wilson grew up as a frail young boy who wasn't great in school. He didn't like sports or reading. What he liked was founding organizations and making rules.

In other words, this guy was the model for every nosy low-level bureaucrat who would follow him. If the DMV had existed in his day, Wilson probably would have gone there for fun. He was the type of guy who, when a meeting was almost over and the leader asks whether there are any further questions, sticks his hand up and talks for another twenty minutes. He was, as my kids might put it, *the absolute worst*.

For the next few decades, as Wilson worked his way up the ladder at various colleges, he became extremely interested in the inner workings of the American government. Specifically, he studied how he might *change* that government so that it operated in a way that pleased him. During one of his many long, dry academic papers on the subject, he wrote, "The Declaration of Independence did not mention the questions of our day. It is of no consequence to us."[1] Like many academics, he thought he could design something better.

Rather than the careful system of checks and balances that had been the hallmark of this great experiment and had sustained the United States government for more than a century by that point, Wilson envisioned a vast bureaucracy of experts: We The People would be scuttled for They The Experts™. He wanted a government that was run primarily by experts—people who, as he put it in one of his landmark books, should have "large powers and unhampered discretion." For Wilson, according to a recent study by the Heritage Foundation, "Administration is properly the province of scientific experts in the bureaucracy. The competence of these experts in the special technological means required to achieve those ends on which we are all agreed gives them the authority to administer or regulate progress unhindered by those within the realm of politics."[2] Reading this today, it's difficult not to think of all the trust-the-science maniacs we were forced to deal with during the Covid-19 pandemic.

Now, coming from an academic, which is what Woodrow Wilson was for most of his adult life, ideas about completely restructuring the American government are pretty innocuous. Coming up with strange theories that have no bearing on the lives of real people is, in some sense, what academics do.

But things changed in 1913, when Woodrow Wilson went from

governor of New Jersey to president of the United States and began attempting to put his wacky progressive ideas into practice. From the White House, President Wilson laid the groundwork for many of the progressive initiatives that would explode under the presidency of Franklin Delano Roosevelt, whose New Deal famously remade the American government according to the whims of those on the far Left.

At first, things moved slowly. As the scholar Charles J. Cooper pointed out in the journal *National Affairs* in February 2015 (shortly before the Obama Administration finalized the Clean Power Plan), there was "an implicit bargain" in place during the New Deal. Agencies such as the Food and Drug Administration, the Environmental Protection Agency, and the Securities and Exchange Commission could exercise legislative and judicial authority because they were staffed by "experts" who, we were told, knew what they were doing. But there were limits.

"The Court," Cooper writes, "would permit Congress to delegate—and the administrative state to exercise—legislative, executive, and judicial power, but it would review administrative exercises of such power to prevent lawlessness and abuse. Judicial review, then, was substituted for the Constitution's checks and balances as the principal safeguard against the administrative state's becoming despotic."[3]

This regime held for a few decades. But slowly, the United States Congress—which has, historically, never been great about dealing with the gray areas and complex questions that might arise from disputes about legislation—gradually began ceding its power to these federal agencies. In one sense, they did this because it was easier than making the laws themselves. It also kept them from having to deal with the consequences of laws that people didn't like. Eventually, the Supreme Court was going to begin treating these agencies like the immensely powerful entities they had become.

This finally happened in 1984, when the Supreme Court heard

a case called *Chevron v. Natural Resources Defense Council.* On its face, the case wasn't terribly interesting. It concerned a regulation by the EPA that claimed it had the authority to interpret vague language in the Clean Air Act to define "stationary source" as an entire plant rather than individual emissions units. In a sense, the outcome wasn't terribly interesting. What *was* interesting was a new rule that emerged from the case—one that amounted, in the words of Charles Cooper, to a renegotiation of the agreement the justices had struck with the Administrative State during the New Deal.

The decision, as he puts it, held that:

> *a court's review of an agency's statutory interpretation proceeds in two steps. First, if the language of the statute is unambiguous, "that is the end of the matter; for the court, as well as the agency, must give effect to the unambiguously expressed intent of Congress." But, if the statute is "silent or unambiguous with respect to the specific issue," the agency's interpretation will be upheld if it is "based on a permissible construction of the statute," even if it is not the construction that the court, using "traditional tools of statutory construction," would adopt. The Court, in true Wilsonian fashion, justified deferring to agency statutory interpretations on the ground that "judges are not experts in the field," whereas agencies can take account of "views of wise policy" in determining the meaning of the statute.*

Suddenly the Administrative State had the power to write laws, and courts couldn't stop them. Whenever a law was deemed ambiguous—which is very often, given the broad language of many federal statutes—a federal agency could simply make up their own rules and force millions of Americans to follow them. In my opinion, and in the opinion of hundreds of other conservative legal scholars who have studied this issue in far more depth than I have, the "*Chevron* doctrine" (as this way of interpreting statutes came to be known) needed to be overturned.

But Supreme Court decisions can't be overturned immediately. Unlike federal agencies, the Court does not simply decree laws from on high. The justices hear the facts of specific cases. And usually, when those cases have made it as far as the Supreme Court, the facts are extremely complicated. As anyone who followed the progress of the various attempts to overturn *Roe v. Wade* over the years knows, it can take a long time for the right case to come around. Over the years, I joined many conservative lawyers in searching for a case that would once again put the conflict between the Administrative State and the people before the Supreme Court.

The search was long. There were few rays of hope. It wasn't until *West Virginia v. EPA* came along that I began to see a chance to make a dent in the *Chevron* doctrine. So, when the Supreme Court announced that it would finally hear *West Virginia v. EPA*, I was elated. Right away, my team and I moved to file a petition along with West Virginia asking the court to take up the case. It read, in part, "This Court's intervention is necessary to clarify that Congress, not administrative agencies, must make major decisions of vast economic and political significance, as the Constitution requires."

On June 30, 2022, we got exactly the outcome we'd been hoping for. While most media outlets in the United States flipped out over the anticipated ruling in *Dobbs v. Jackson Women's Health Organization*, which finally overturned *Roe v. Wade*, we in the conservative legal community had our own small celebration over the outcome of the *EPA* case. Finally the Supreme Court had taken a step in curtailing the Administrative State's power, signaling a shift away from the long-standing *Chevron* doctrine and replacing it with a more restrictive standard under the major-questions doctrine. Writing for the majority, Chief Justice John Roberts declared, "It is not plausible that Congress gave EPA the authority to adopt on its own such

a regulatory scheme. . . . A decision of such magnitude and consequence rests with Congress itself, or an agency acting pursuant to a
clear delegation from that representative body."

In a concurring opinion, Justice Neil Gorsuch—who had
long sought to overturn the blatantly unconstitutional *Chevron*
doctrine—told the story in the clear prose for which he's become
famous on the court. In outlining the new major-questions doctrine,
he explained:

> Under the doctrine's terms, administrative agencies must be
> able to point to "clear congressional authorization" when they
> claim the power to make decision of vast "economic and political
> significance." . . . One of the Judiciary's most solemn duties is to
> ensure that acts of Congress are applied in accordance with the
> Constitution in the cases that come before us. To help fulfill that
> duty, courts have developed certain "clear-statement" rules. These
> rules assume that, absent a clear statement otherwise, Congress
> means for its laws to operate in congruence with the Constitution
> rather than test its bounds. In this way, these clear-statement rules
> help courts "act as faithful agents of the Constitution."

The decision didn't go all the way in eliminating *Chevron*. But
it *was* the largest dent in that long-standing doctrine's armor that
we had seen in many years. I was proud to have played a role, however small, in such a seismic shift in American law. In addition to
the benefits for future cases that sought to curtail the power of the
Administrative State, there were very real benefits to the people of
Missouri, as well as the American people in general. Thanks to the
court's ruling in the *EPA* case, the legal ground was set for a decision soon thereafter, in which the Court would formally overrule the
Chevron doctrine.

Still, we continued to look for the perfect set of facts that could overturn *Chevron*. What we would need, I knew, was a case in which it was clear that a federal agency had reached a decision in interpreting an ambiguous statute that the courts probably would not have reached, and someone who was directly injured by this decision would be willing to stand up to the Administrative State and challenge their unchecked power. In many ways, this was the "white whale" of the conservative legal community. In the end, I wasn't the one who ended up getting that case.

But the plaintiffs in *Loper Bright Enterprises v. Raimondo* sure did.

Chapter 12

THE CASE I ALWAYS WANTED

As I mentioned in the last chapter, finding a case that could overturn *Chevron* deference was, effectively, the white whale of the conservative legal community. For years I was Captain Ahab, leaning over the side of my boat, searching for movement in the water in the hope that I might be the one to reel it in.

Of course, that didn't happen for me.

But I think it's only fitting that the case that finally *did* overturn *Chevron* deference began on the water. Specifically, with fishing boats, and a rule requiring fishing companies to pay for federal monitors—that is, government cops—to ride on these boats and ensure compliance with the thousands of government regulations pertaining to the fishing industry.

One of these companies was Loper Bright Enterprises, a regional fishing company that had been operating in New England for many years. Looking at the facts of the case, their frustration was understandable. In essence, the government (specifically the National Marine Fisheries Service, or NMFS), was telling the company that they needed to foot the bill for a government office that would look over their shoulders and make sure they were complying with the government's own regulations. It's as if the Internal Revenue Service were to tell you that you needed to pay to have one of their agents live in a small bedroom in your house, just to look over your receipts every few days and ensure you were classifying them in the right way.

From the moment the case was filed in February 2020, I took

notice. So did many other conservative legal scholars. On its face, the case seemed perfect. However, at the time, we weren't sure that the Supreme Court had the right composition to get us a favorable ruling. Back then, there was still only a 5–4 conservative majority on the court. If just one justice went the other way and sided with the liberals (which some of them often did), the whole thing could have been blown, and we might have been stuck with the *Chevron* deference doctrine for another forty years.

As the case worked its way up from the district court through the appeals process, I decided that my team in Missouri would play our own small role in paving the way for the overturning of *Chevron*. In part, that meant attracting like-minded legal talent from all over the country. Almost as soon as I took office, I brought in people who knew regulations inside and out, and who shared the same dream of ending *Chevron* deference. I also instructed my staff not to make any deference arguments in defense of state regulations. This meant that the state equivalent of the *Chevron* doctrine was effectively dead in Missouri, because the Missouri Attorney General would not invoke the doctrine in defending state regulations. By controlling what we did and did not argue, we were able to prevent our office from expanding the *Chevron* doctrine in state courts.

I also played a little offense. Early on in my first year, I got word that several municipalities in Missouri were issuing ticket quotas for their police departments. In effect, this was "taxation by citation," and it represented the same kind of government overreach we were trying to fight in the cases about *Chevron* deference. This was a fight I had been carrying on since I first got into public service, and I believed it was important to continue it from the AG's office.

Back in 2014, in the aftermath of what happened in Ferguson, Missouri, I met with community leaders and police officers to ask what my colleagues and I might be able to do to help. I was in the Missouri Senate at the time, trying to collaborate on legislation that would make real differences in people's lives, however small. Quickly I learned that trust between the people and the police—and people and their courts—was suffering as well. It turns out local bureaucrats were pushing their police departments to issue traffic tickets to raise revenue. The cops I talked to were frustrated as well. They'd tell me they didn't go to the police academy to write traffic tickets all day long, but in some municipalities their jobs depended on the revenue they generated for politicians and bureaucrats. This was wrong.

It didn't take long to figure out what was going on. St. Ann is a suburb of St. Louis just a few miles from where I grew up that had once been home to the largest shopping mall in the country before Mall of America came along in Minnesota. As the St. Ann mall faded in viability, so did the tax receipts. So, to plug up the gaps, local officials leaned on police departments to write more traffic tickets. As I would point out in an op-ed on the subject published in *The Wall Street Journal*, "Between 2009 and 2014, St. Ann's police department went from writing 3,500 tickets worth $722,000 to 10,000 tickets worth $2,834,000."[1]

It got worse.

To quote myself again:

Next door in Edmundson, a town of fewer than 1,000 people, Mayor John Gwaltney wrote an April 2014 letter to his city's police, noting a "marked downturn in traffic and other tickets being written by your department." The mayor went on to remind officers that the tickets they write add to the revenue on which the police department budget is established, "and will directly affect pay adjustments at budget time." Mayor Gwaltney had a subtle way of delivering his message: The letter was included with police officers' paychecks.

So, in 2015 I filed legislation in the General Assembly that put a low cap on the amount of revenue that municipalities in Missouri could generate from traffic tickets and fines, among other reforms. Later, we'd ban traffic ticket quotas as well. Law enforcement, community leaders, and even the ACLU supported the bill. Local government folks opposed it, but it passed overwhelmingly. It was the most significant legislation to come from what was to be known across the country as "Ferguson" and represented the most significant municipal law reform in Missouri history. It was also an important step toward shifting some power away from the government bureaucrats and back to the people.

By the time I became Attorney General of Missouri, that legislation was still in place. However, I began hearing reports that some municipalities were still engaging in "taxation by citation" schemes. Every time it happened, my office quickly filed suit. One of the most egregious cases happened in Moscow Mills, Missouri, where a chief in the police department was accused of instructing his traffic enforcement officer to "write at least ten citations per day" and instructed other officers "to write 160 citations per month, excluding December and January, to annually secure $160,000 in citation revenue."[2] Immediately we sent a letter demanding that the department cease and desist from this practice. It worked, just as it had in the nearby cities of Diamond and Marshfield. Diamond, the first city that I sued, had blatantly advertised its illegal policies on the police department whiteboard: "We R $5,000 B hind issue some tickets RFN." RFN stood for "right [expletive] now."

Although this might seem like it has little to do with the more overarching mission of overturning the doctrine of *Chevron* deference, the two are more closely linked than you might imagine. In taking on these fights, I was attempting to create a new model for state Attorneys General: We would take on government overreach at all levels—federal, state and local. I wanted to transfer power away from unelected bureaucrats and back toward the people. In 2020, when several municipalities in Missouri voted to disband their police departments in closed sessions, I brought successful lawsuits against them and won. In the grand scheme of things, these were small developments. But taken as a whole it was a comprehensive strategy guided by conservative principles and executed in a way that hadn't been done before.

*

While I was working on these fights in Missouri, President Trump was waging battles of his own from the White House. From the moment he began his first term, he worked with members of his Administration to remove burdensome government regulations that prevented businesses from flourishing (something he is doing right now during his second term). He also came into office in 2017 with a vacancy on the Supreme Court. And as we saw in the last chapter, the man knew how to pick judges. One of his first was Neil Gorsuch, a federal judge from Denver who had taken a bold stance on *Chevron* deference in the past. During his confirmation hearing, Representative Jerrod Nadler of New York lambasted Judge Gorsuch, saying, "You would destroy the ability of Congress to legislate and agencies to administer, and you'd have no predictability for citizens to anticipate what they can and can't do. There's no way Congress can anticipate every situation or rule in every situation. That's why we set out broad rules."

In reality, the judicial philosophy espoused by Gorsuch and other legal conservatives would have exactly the opposite effect. In the absence of excessive deference to federal agencies, it would become crystal clear what the laws mean. Anything that aligned with the United States Constitution would be permitted, and anything that did not would be forbidden. Watching the confirmation hearings, I could tell that the most left-wing members of Congress were terrified of Judge Gorsuch, as well as any other Supreme Court appointees made by President Trump. That, I figured, was a good sign.

Over the next four years, President Trump nominated two more justices to the Supreme Court, fundamentally changing the makeup of our judiciary at the highest level. Finally, the configuration that the conservative legal community had been waiting for was in place. And it happened just in time for *Loper Bright Enterprises v. Raimondo* to go before the court. Rather than making small dents in the Administrative State in the way we'd been doing for the past few decades, the decision in this case would shatter the doctrine of *Chevron* deference once and for all.

As soon as the opinion came out in the summer of 2024, it was clear that we had experienced a complete shift in our legal system. By this time I had been a United States Senator for a year and a half, working from inside the halls of Congress to write clear laws that would keep the power of the Administrative State in check. I was elated to hear that the Supreme Court had finally reversed its decision in *Chevron v. National Resources Council*, calling the *Chevron* doctrine "fundamentally misguided." It was even more heartening to see that Chief Justice John Roberts sided with five other justices on the case, and that only Justices Elena Kagan, Sonia Sotomayor, and Ketanji Brown Jackson dissented, arguing that the *Chevron* doctrine provided necessary deference to agencies on complex, technical matters beyond Congress's expertise.

In many ways, the ruling felt like the culmination of a movement. Finally we had landed a fatal blow against those who believed, like Woodrow Wilson and the other progressives of the early twentieth century, that our government should be run primarily by unelected "experts." It is worth nothing that Chief Justice Roberts, attempting to preempt those objections, noted that "Congress expects courts to handle technical statutory questions," and that courts are more than capable of doing so.

Now in the U.S. Senate I'm continuing this work by leading the post-*Chevron* working group, and we have made recommendations on how to codify greater accountability measures for bureaucrats, give less deference to agencies, and provide ways the Article I branch can write laws more clearly. In the end, the American people deserve accountability in the government, and recent conservative legal wins have given them just that.

Chapter 13

THE STUDENT LOAN
FORGIVENESS SCAM

When kids run for class president, they often make big promises. One kid would say there'd be pizza parties every Friday; another kid would promise to replace school lunches with Happy Meals from McDonald's. The teachers would look on from the back of the auditorium and laugh, knowing that not a single person would be able to remember who ended up winning the election at all.

Something similar happened in the middle of Joe Biden's first (and only) term in office. Sensing that he was losing the support of the people, Biden got together with his advisors and cooked up the closest thing to a pizza-party-on-Fridays promise that I've seen in modern political history. He stood in the Oval Office and announced that he was taking unilateral action to wipe away anywhere from $500 billion to $1 trillion in student loan debt. That amounted to $20,000 in cold, hard cash to each individual with unpaid debt. In a speech in August 2022, he framed the move in dire language, attempting to convince us he was the hero we'd been waiting for and this was an "emergency."

"The burden is so heavy," he said,

that even if you graduate, you may not have access to the middle-class life that the college degree once provided. Many people—many people can't qualify for a mortgage to buy a home because the debt they continue to carry. They—you know, they carry—it's too high. They can't come up with a down payment anyway. A lot of folks are even putting off starting families because of the cost. And the dream of starting or owning your business is just way off in the distance with a debt that's—that so many are saddled with. Many of you had to leave school because the financial strain was much too high. About a third of the borrowers have debt but no degree and—worst of both worlds: debt and no degree. The burden is especially heavy on Black and Hispanic borrowers, who on average have less family wealth to pay for it. There's no—they don't own their homes to borrow against to be able to pay for college.

This time, the playbook wasn't going to work. Even many on the Left could see that this student debt cancellation was nothing more than a cynical ploy to win the votes of young, cash-strapped borrowers before the midterm elections. As someone who paid a small fortune in student loan bills, I understood how frustrating the process could be. My family and I put off making major financial decisions because I had to pay off the debt I had incurred; many of our friends did the same thing.

Watching Biden's announcement, I couldn't help think of all my friends, cousins, and others growing up who had decided not to go to college because they couldn't pay for it. Rather than take out big loans the way I did, they made different decisions. Some paid for school as they went. Some went to some college. Some went to technical schools. Some got jobs as truck drivers, HVAC technicians, and laborers. They learned trades that enabled them to make good livings for their families. All that time, they had paid their taxes, expecting that the money they sent to the government would pay for essential services such as infrastructure, public transportation, and education for their children. Now Joe Biden was telling those people that their tax dollars would be used to pay off the debt of all the people who had taken out loans to go to college and no longer wanted to pay for it.

It was outrageous. And I wasn't the only one who thought so. As soon as the policy was floated by the Biden Administration, many prominent Republicans came out against it. Like me, they didn't think it was remotely fair that truck drivers and waitresses were going to pay the unpaid loan debt of some tenured theater professor at Harvard University who doesn't want to make his payments anymore.

But the options for fighting Biden's proposal were limited, and it didn't seem like there was anything Congress could do to stop him. During a RAGA meeting around this time, a few other Republican AGs and I discussed potential legal avenues to fight it. Once again, the law was on our side. No law or statute gave Joe Biden the authority to wipe away at least $500 billion in student loan debt, so the gambit was plainly unlawful. But this was a federal issue. For the moment, it seemed, there was nothing that could be done at the state level to stop it. A few AGs suggested suing on behalf of taxpayers, claiming that they would be harmed by having their tax dollars so grossly misused.

I liked the general thrust of the idea, but it didn't seem like it would be successful. Sometimes, when you're dealing with such egregious abuses of power at the federal level, you need to think creatively.

So, after a long brainstorming session, that's exactly what I did.

*

In the state of Missouri, there is a loan-servicing agency called the Missouri Higher Education Loan Authority, or MOHELA. It's a quasi-state agency—part of the Missouri government. Most people have never heard of it. I, on the other hand, knew the organization well. For over a decade they had been in charge of my student loan debt. To this day I can remember the look of the envelopes that used to come to my house.

Rather than suing on behalf of taxpayers, which seemed like a dicey proposition to me, I thought we could sue on behalf of MOHELA, allowing us to tell a single, specific story in the courtroom. The logic was simple. Like most loan servicers, MOHELA made its money by collecting interest on loans; if those loans were illegally forgiven by Joe Biden, they would lose money and maybe go out of business. I would be suing on behalf of the people of Missouri, but I would be doing it in a way that gave me a much greater chance of success.

Some of my most trusted political advisors didn't agree. By this point I had won the primary for an open U.S. Senate seat in Missouri. The race was tight, and it was really going to start heating up over the next few months. One of my advisors told me not to rock the boat. The politics of this issue weren't yet clear; for all we knew, student debt forgiveness might turn out to be popular even among the voters I was trying to win over. But I had a feeling that the case, however strange the details might have been, was a winner—not to mention that I believed it was the right thing to do.

So, we wrote up a complaint that put my legal theory into practice. Michael Talent, a legal prodigy working in my office, was the one who crafted the finer points of the theory and eventually wrote the winning briefs. It was straightforward: The Biden Administration's move to forgive these loans would directly harm MOHELA, a Missouri state entity, which in turn harmed the taxpayers. This harm was key to getting us standing in court, and from there it was up to the judges to decide if the President's power play would hold up. We had Nebraska join since they were another Eight Circuit state and I loved working with Doug Peterson, their Attorney General—he was a great guy and had a good team.

Then came the Left's objections. They knew this case could come down to standing and MOHELA was the hook (they were right), so they wanted MOHELA out. They said MOHELA was an unwilling client and that this whole suit was politically motivated. But as Attorney General, I represented the entirety of my state's interests whether the bureaucrats at MOHELA wanted me to sue Joe Biden or not. I wasn't elected to back down when the stakes were high.

We fought hard in the courts, all the way to the Supreme Court, to halt an overreach that would burden future generations with half a trillion dollars in debt forgiveness that the Constitution had never permitted. The Biden Administration argued that the HEROES Act of 2003 granted it the authority to cancel $500 billion in federal student debt, citing provisions allowing the secretary of education to "waive or modify" student financial assistance programs during national emergencies. But as we argued, and the Court confirmed, this interpretation stretched far beyond the Act's intended purpose—to provide flexibility for service members and affected borrowers in times of temporary hardship, not to enact sweeping economic policy.

In the majority opinion, Chief Justice John Roberts scrutinized the Administration's rationale. He wrote, "The Secretary's power under the HEROES Act to 'waive or modify' does not remotely authorize such a vast and transformative policy." Roberts pointed out that if Congress had intended such a sweeping delegation of power to the executive branch, it would have done so clearly. Instead, Congress had chosen language that supported only modest changes, not the wholesale cancellation of debt for millions of borrowers. No amount of legal reinterpretation could transform a narrow provision into a blank check.

The court also noted that if an executive branch official wanted to make such sweeping changes, it was up to Congress to legislate them directly—a principle firmly rooted in the major-questions doctrine, which requires clear congressional authorization for actions of "vast economic and political significance." In this case, as Roberts noted, "the economic and political significance of the Department's action is staggering by any measure."

It was a big win, and if MOHELA hadn't been a plaintiff this challenge would have been tossed for lack of standing. Democrats knew it then and know it now, which is why they are trying to put it out of business even today.

After the decision, Biden tried to defy the Court. He said his plan was derailed by "MAGA Republicans" and "special interests." He went on to say in a speech in Culver City, California, "The Supreme Court blocked it, but that didn't stop me." He was alluding to other later attempts to do forgive student loan debt, but he lost and he lost badly. I am proud to say that I actually saved taxpayers over half a trillion dollars.

This was a win not just for Missouri or for those of us who stood up to fight, but for every American who is weary of Permanent Washington's constant efforts to expand its authority beyond what was authorized by law. The decision sent a message loud and clear: When citizens and states challenge executive overreach, we can secure a victory for constitutional governance. It reaffirmed a critical principle of our republic: that power belongs closer to the people, with their elected representatives, not with unelected officials interpreting statutes beyond their scope.

Part V

Defending the Second Amendment

Chapter 14

STICKING TO OUR GUNS

Among his many good qualities, Justice Antonin Scalia was a master of making the law clear and accessible for everyone. Anyone can read his opinions and follow the complex lines of argument he's crafting. There is perhaps no better example of this than the majority opinion he wrote in *District of Columbia v. Heller.*

The case, which reached the Supreme Court in 2005, involved a police officer named Dick Heller who sought to keep a handgun in his home for self-defense. Heller, permitted to carry a gun while on duty, applied for a registration certificate to keep the firearm at home. However, the District of Columbia denied his application, citing its stringent gun control law that prohibited private citizens from possessing handguns at home. This denial led Heller to challenge the law, arguing that it violated his Second Amendment rights to bear arms for self-protection.

Under a more permissive Supreme Court, things might have gone differently for Heller. It was exactly the kind of case that a left-wing justice would have looked at as an opportunity to do a little legislating from the bench. Given the prevalence of crimes involving a firearm—which, on the Left, you might call an "emergency"—a left-wing Court might have upheld the ruling by the D.C. Circuit, determining that the right to bear arms did not extend to private citizens. This would have involved a deliberate misreading of the Constitution. But as we've seen in previous chapters, deliberate misreadings of the

Constitution are as common on the Left as trigger warnings and DEI struggle sessions.

Luckily, the American people had enough justices on the Court who were willing to stand up to political pressure, which was a tough thing to do at the time. Even in 2005, there were calls every day to toss out the Second Amendment and ban guns entirely. Advocates for this course of action didn't care *how* we banned guns; they just wanted it done quickly. And, as often happens, they turned to the Supreme Court, hoping that the justices would once again legislate from the bench and make the right to bear arms a thing of the past.

Justice Scalia took a different approach. Rather than taking stock of what the popular thing to do might have been, he turned to our history, and the history of the right to bear arms in general. Over the course of a few months, he combed through documents that dated back to the days before the United States of America had even been founded.

The lessons they learned are apparent in the opinion that Justice Scalia eventually produced. Reading it today, you can get a master class in legal reasoning and the art of plain rhetoric. First, Justice Scalia notes that "in interpreting [the Second Amendment], we are guided by the principle that the Constitution was written to be understood by the voters; its words and phrases were used in their normal and ordinary as distinguished from technical meaning." Although this might seem straightforward to some readers, it was something that needed to be said at the time. For too long, legal scholars on the Left had been insisting that original public meaning and the intent of the founders didn't matter, or that it mattered less than what the people of the United States might want in the present moment. Aside from being an improper way to read the United States Constitution on philosophical grounds, this approach was wrongheaded because it assumed that societies always get better with age—something that any student of history knows is not true. If you still believe it, take a look at the fall of Rome, or many twentieth century European countries.

As several conservative legal scholars have pointed out over the years, a government means nothing if it doesn't have a structure at its center. And that structure, bounded by the Constitution, cannot waver as the times change, unless the people decide to change it. Even when Congress passes laws according to the will of the people, they can't violate the Constitution. And the Second Amendment—which, other than the First, is probably the one that has come under attack most often from the Left—is about as clear as it gets.

It reads:

> *A well regulated militia, being necessary to the security of a free State, the right of the people to keep and bear Arms, shall not be infringed.*

Of course, *clear* might not be the best word. To modern ears, there's something a little jarring about the language. If you paid attention in high school English, you might even recognize that the first part of the sentence may seem to some to not quite line up with the second part. But according to the Supreme Court's opinion in *District of Columbia v. Heller*, even that has a purpose. The first part, as it says on page one of the opinion, "does not limit the latter grammatically, but rather announces a purpose. The amendment could be rephrased, 'Because a well regulated Militia is necessary to the security of a free state, the right of the people to keep and bear arms shall not be infringed.' Although the structure of the Second Amendment is unique in our Constitution, other legal documents, of the Founding era, particularly individual-rights provisions of state constitutions, commonly included a prefatory statement of purpose."

The amendment is unique in other ways. For one thing, it doesn't say "the people shall have the right to keep and bear arms." It says that the right of the people to keep and bear arms *shall not be infringed*. It is phrased this way because the founders knew they were not giving the right to bear arms to the people. Governments, in their minds, couldn't do that. The right to bear arms, just like the right to free speech, comes from God, and it was the job of the United States government to protect that right.

For centuries, this was a tradition. People understood the profound importance of the right to keep and bear arms because history had shown them, time and again, the dangers of a government unchecked by its people. Governments in those days were often embodied by kings or tyrants, figures who ruled with an iron fist and little regard for individual freedoms. In 1686, for instance, the Stuart Kings of England—James II in particular—began a campaign to disarm certain groups of citizens, particularly Protestants, under the guise of "maintaining order" and "protecting peace." This wasn't a simple matter of confiscating a few weapons here and there; it was a calculated effort to strip power from those the king deemed politically or religiously threatening. James II believed that a disarmed populace was a compliant one, easier to manage and far less likely to rebel against the Crown's increasingly authoritarian rule.

This act of disarmament was part of a broader, oppressive agenda. The Stuart Kings aimed to centralize their power, weaken Parliament, and eliminate any potential threats to their rule. But the people saw through it. They knew that losing the right to bear arms meant losing a critical means of defending their freedoms, property, and, ultimately, their lives. This realization fueled the tensions that would culminate in the Glorious Revolution of 1688, where James II was overthrown and Parliament reinstated protections for individual liberties. Among these protections was an acknowledgment of the right to bear arms, later enshrined in the 1689 English Bill of Rights.

It wasn't only the English. In France during the 1700s, Louis XIV and his successors imposed harsh restrictions on firearms. As discontent simmered, French kings actively disarmed peasants and other groups to prevent uprisings against the monarchy. They knew that a populace unable to defend itself was a populace more likely to obey, and they feared the consequences of armed dissent, particularly as the ideals of liberty and equality began to spread. And, of course, King George III took the same approach with the American colonies when they began getting out of line. In the wake of the Boston Tea Party and other acts of defiance, British officials attempted to confiscate colonial arms to keep the colonists from further resistance. This effort culminated in the British attempt to seize a stockpile of weapons at Concord, Massachusetts, in 1775, an action that sparked the first battles of the American Revolutionary War. The British sought to prevent armed resistance, but the colonists understood that without the means to defend themselves, they would lose more than their arms—they would lose their freedoms.

That is why the Second Amendment was so important to our founding fathers. They remembered what it was like to have a tyrannical government that wanted to disarm them, and they wanted to make sure that no matter how the political winds changed—no matter how many people grew fearful of guns, or how many tragedies certain political parties attempted to blame on the freedom to purchase guns—that the right to bear arms could not be taken away simply because a simple majority of people wanted it to happen. Once again, the Bill of Rights exists to protect a minority from, as James Madison put it in Federalist 51, the "tyranny of the majority."

Still, we've seen many attempts over the years to disarm the people of the United States. Largely, these have come from the political Left, which has come to view crimes committed by armed criminals—just like everything else it dislikes—as a "national emergency" that must be remedied by extreme (and immediate) government intervention.

In 1968, for example, Congress passed the Gun Control Act in the wake of high-profile assassinations, expanding federal control over firearms and banning interstate sales of guns. The act restricted access to firearms for various groups and imposed greater licensing requirements, setting the stage for a broader push to limit individual ownership rights.

In 1975, the District of Columbia passed the Firearms Control Regulations Act—the law at the heart of the *Heller* case. This strict legislation effectively banned private handgun ownership within the city by prohibiting residents from registering new handguns and requiring that legally owned firearms, such as rifles and shotguns, be kept unloaded and either disassembled or secured with a trigger lock. The law meant that even in one's own home, a resident couldn't keep a loaded, operable gun for self-defense, effectively eliminating the right to personal protection within the home.

For years, these laws went relatively unchallenged at the Supreme Court. Despite the fact that they clearly violated the Second Amendment to our Constitution, justices were willing to live with these laws because they seemed to serve a public good according to their worldview. It wasn't until 2005, when the *Heller* case was taken up by a mostly originalist court, that things changed. Considering the question of whether the words "bear arms" extended to private ownership of handguns in the home, Justice Scalia wrote:

> [T]he inherent right of self-defense has been central to the Second Amendment right. The [District of Columbia's] handgun ban amounts to a prohibition of an entire class of "arms" that is overwhelmingly chosen by American society for that lawful purpose. The prohibition extends, moreover, to the home, where the need for defense of self, family, and property is most acute. Under any of the standards of scrutiny that we have applied to enumerated constitutional rights, banning from the home "the most preferred

firearm in the nation to keep and use for protection of one's home and family" would fail constitutional muster.

The very enumeration of the right takes out of the hands of government—even the Third Branch of Government—the power to decide on a case-by-case basis whether the right is really worth insisting upon. A constitutional guarantee subject to future judges' assessments of its usefulness is no constitutional guarantee at all. Constitutional rights are enshrined with the scope they were understood to have when the people adopted them, whether or not future legislatures or (yes) even future judges think that scope too broad.

In other words, the right to bear arms does not stop existing because judges of a particular political persuasion want it to. Rather, it is the job of judges to make sure that state legislatures and the United States Congress do not make laws that violate that right, even when doing so is unpopular. At the time that the *Heller* opinion came down, this was seen by many as a radical view. Liberals hated it.

The passage of time, however, has revealed *Heller* to be one of the most important opinions in the history of judicial conservatism. It's no wonder that Randy Barnett, a law professor at Georgetown University, called it "sweeping and masterful," writing that it served as "the culmination of his ambition to place the original meaning of the text at the center of constitutional law."[1] When I first read the opinion as a recent graduate of law school, I remember thinking how well reasoned it was and how it cut to the heart of why individual liberty must be protected. The same went for many of the opinions that came down during the Scalia years. But I also knew, even then, that this kind of legal reasoning was only possible when the right judges were on the right benches. Otherwise a permissive attitude would take over, and laws that curtailed the freedom of the American people would be allowed to remain on the books.

Sadly, the next few years proved me right. During the Obama era, we saw the nomination of two Supreme Court justices—Sonia Sotomayor and Elena Kagan—whose judicial philosophies diverged dramatically from those of originalists. Their influence was evident in rulings such as *Arizona v. United States* (2012) and *National Federation of Independent Business v. Sebelius* (2012), both of which expanded federal authority at the expense of states' rights and the original meaning of the Constitution.

In *Arizona v. United States*, the court struck down key provisions of Arizona's immigration law, S.B. 1070, which allowed state law enforcement to assist in enforcing federal immigration laws. The majority ruled that the federal government had preemptive authority over immigration, dismissing the fact that states like Arizona bear much of the burden of illegal immigration. This decision undermined the Tenth Amendment and restricted the states' power to defend their own borders and protect their citizens from the economic and security impacts of unlawful immigration.

In *National Federation of Independent Business v. Sebelius*, the court upheld the Affordable Care Act's individual mandate by redefining it as a tax, despite Congress framing it as a penalty. This ruling not only expanded federal reach into individual decision-making but also disregarded the clear, original limits of Congress's taxing and commerce powers. Upholding the individual mandate under these terms distorted the enumerated powers of Congress, which were never intended to allow for sweeping, coercive control over Americans' health care choices.

These cases exemplified a broader trend in the court during this period: interpreting the Constitution as a "living document" to accommodate modern policy goals rather than adhering to the text's original meaning. This approach not only eroded states' rights but also paved the way for expansive federal authority that runs counter to the constitutional structure intended by the framers. And it wasn't just the courts. Seeing this permissive attitude take hold in our court system, several states and cities began attempting to curtail the Second Amendment via onerous laws and regulations, making it so hard to obtain and carry firearms that the right to bear arms might as well not exist at all.

If you were on the political Left and didn't fully appreciate our constitutional structure and protections, you might want to "take action" to address the violence in the streets, and so guns are an easy target. Just like the Covid-19 lockdowns, these measures made them feel like they were "doing something." They also pleased the media and the Democratic donor base. But that didn't change the fact that unless we vote to repeal the Second Amendment—something that would need to be approved by Congress and three-quarters of the States—it remains unconstitutional to infringe upon the right of the people to keep and bear arms. And amending the Constitution to repeal the Second Amendment would take away one of our most important liberties and bastions against tyranny.

Of course, there are some lawmakers and local officials who don't care very much about what is and is not constitutional. In many cases, they only want to put laws on the books so it looks like they're doing something to solve the "national emergency" of "gun violence." These include regulations—some sensible, others not— about who can possess a firearm. They include the implementation of "gun-free zones" where people are prohibited from carrying weapons in their own defense.

As Attorney General of Missouri, I saw it as part of my job to watch out for clear violations of the Second Amendment so that we could fight them in court. Just because those laws weren't being put in place in Missouri didn't mean I still couldn't stand up for the rights of Americans in the courtroom. It simply meant that we needed to be entrepreneurial.

So, when I heard there was a case challenging New York's

burdensome process to obtain a concealed carry permit, I knew we needed to step in. And once again, I wasn't the only one who thought so. Other states, primarily Arizona, were interested in designing a strategy that would allow us to prevail at the Supreme Court, thereby protecting the Second Amendment right of Americans everywhere. Before I describe that strategy and how we came up with it, I feel it's important to say a little about one of the reasons the case and why it mattered so much to me—and why it *should* matter to every citizen of the United States.

*

Many cities suffered during the Covid-19 pandemic. Crime rates skyrocketed. People were out of work. In many cases, the police felt that they couldn't enforce the law because doing so might land them in hot water with the radical Left. I know this happened in Missouri, where cities like St. Louis and Kansas City experienced significant increases in violent crime rates, and law enforcement agencies faced challenges due to disastrous budget cuts and retirements due to disrespect from Democrats and radical activists on the streets and worse.

But there was perhaps no major city that had it worse than New York City, where Mayor Bill de Blasio and his liberal allies had been driving policies that weakened law enforcement, emboldened criminals, and stifled the rights of ordinary citizens to defend themselves. By the time the Covid-19 pandemic rolled around—bringing with it roving mobs of left-wing agitators, calls to "defund the police," and an escalating sense of lawlessness—the city was already at a breaking point. Many residents saw firsthand that city officials couldn't (or wouldn't) protect them, and it was no surprise that firearm purchases surged. The number of people applying for firearm permits skyrocketed from 2,400 in 2019 to over 8,000 in 2020, according to the New York City Police Department's License Division. Even in a city with some of the strictest gun control laws in the nation, New Yorkers realized that self-protection was essential as the promise of public safety slipped away.

This was especially important for women. According to a study conducted by the National Rifle Association (NRA), firearm ownership can be the difference between life and death for women, who are disproportionately affected by violent domestic crimes. In the absence of firearms, the physically stronger person has a huge advantage. This was especially true in New York City, where crimes like robbery and assault increased dramatically amid the lawless atmosphere of Covid-19. Unfortunately, firearms had never been harder to acquire in one of the most dangerous cities on earth—for law-abiding citizens, at least.

Thanks to a burdensome regulatory regime that had been instituted, obtaining a firearm was extremely difficult. For one thing, anyone who wanted to get a gun had to demonstrate "proper cause," effectively making the case to some bureaucrat that they faced an imminent and unique danger to their personal safety— something *beyond* the risks the general public experienced. This requirement forced applicants to prove an exceptional need, which meant that simply wanting a firearm for self-defense in a high-crime city wasn't enough. Without the ability to meet this restrictive standard, ordinary citizens were effectively denied the right to carry firearms for self-defense. This issue became the crux of *New York State Rifle & Pistol Association, Inc. v. Bruen*.

Criminals, on the other hand, didn't bother to go through these steps. They just bought guns on the black market as they always had. As *The New York Times* has shown, illegal guns in New York City were more common than ever during the Covid-19 pandemic. Gun crime went up by 97 percent in 2020 compared to the previous year. The same was true in Missouri, where we saw 689 firearm-related homicides during the pandemic. But we didn't happen to have a regulatory regime in Missouri that made obtaining a firearm nearly impossible. New York did.

During a RAGA conference, a few state AGs and I discussed how to proceed. At first there was some jockeying for position. Arizona's AG office, which had been doing commendable work in recent months, believed it should take the lead. But gun rights activists cared a lot too and relationships mattered. Over the years, I had built solid connections with gun rights groups. We had established a foundation of trust, and Missouri was widely regarded as the go-to office on gun policy. Arizona's team presented their angle, which was empirically driven, but we felt it wasn't as strong as the direction we intended to take, which was more of a constitutional analysis.

In the end, we settled on an approach that emphasized both constitutional and empirical grounds, showing how New York's restrictive licensing law infringed on the Second Amendment right to bear arms outside the home. We brought more AGs into the fold, worked through the initial turf battles, and ultimately came out unified, with an amicus brief we could all stand behind.

In our brief, we argued that New York's "proper cause" requirement—an arbitrary standard set by state officials to determine whether an individual could carry a firearm outside the home—was an unconstitutional barrier to a fundamental right. The Second Circuit's ruling "threatens the liberty of citizens in every State, not just New York," we wrote, explaining that "subjective-issue handgun permit regimes ... are unconstitutional because they impose state-created, subjective conditions upon the exercise of a fundamental constitutional right." The Second Amendment, we argued, was not meant to be selectively enforced; rather, it was intended to provide every law-abiding citizen the right to self-defense, irrespective of where they lived or the subjective decisions of local officials.

Our brief then turned to evidence from other states. In states with "shall-issue" licensing systems—where permits are granted based on objective, clear criteria like background checks and training requirements—data showed consistently lower crime or neutral impact on crime. In contrast to New York's "proper cause" standard, these objective systems showed "that homicide rates will not increase as a result of crimes committed by persons with carry permits." This assertion was backed by extensive research on permit holders, who overwhelmingly proved to be more law-abiding than the general population. We emphasized that public safety could be preserved without infringing on individual rights, as evidenced by the success of these shall-issue states.

In addition to modern data, we drew from historical context. Our brief called on the Court to uphold the Second Amendment's original public meaning, citing centuries-old views on the right to self-defense as "central" to American liberty. We argued that self-defense was a core reason for the right to bear arms and cited Alexander Hamilton's words to drive this home. Hamilton argued that a large army would never be needed "while there is a large body of citizens ... who stand ready to defend their own rights and those of their fellow citizens."

In the end, we made a strong case for restoring the right to bear arms outside the home as the founders intended. New York's restrictive approach, we argued, was fundamentally incompatible with both the Constitution's original meaning and with the real-world evidence from other states. Objective licensing regimes respect citizens' rights and enhance public safety by ensuring that responsible, law-abiding individuals can exercise their right to self-defense without arbitrary state interference. We concluded with a call for the court to restore the Second Amendment to its full, original purpose: to protect the rights of citizens to defend themselves and to ensure that no state may infringe upon that right.

On June 23, 2022, the Supreme Court ruled in favor of the

petitioners in *New York State Rifle & Pistol Association, Inc. v. Bruen.*
Writing for the majority, Justice Clarence Thomas emphasized that
the right to bear arms is a fundamental one and should not be treated
differently from other constitutional rights:

> *The Second Amendment is not "a second-class right, subject to
> an entirely different body of rules than the other Bill of Rights
> guarantees." . . . We know of no other constitutional right that an
> individual may exercise only after demonstrating to government
> officers some special need. That is not how the First Amendment
> works when it comes to unpopular speech or the free exercise of
> religion. It is not how the Sixth Amendment works when it comes to
> a defendant's right to confront the witnesses against him. And it is
> not how the Second Amendment works when it comes to public carry
> for self-defense.*

This echoes the argument we made in our amicus brief, which as-
serted that New York's subjective "proper cause" standard unlawfully
placed state-imposed, arbitrary conditions on a fundamental constitutional right. We argued that "subjective-issue handgun permit
regimes . . . are unconstitutional because they impose state-created,
subjective conditions upon the exercise of a fundamental constitutional right." Just as our brief called for the Second Amendment to
receive the same respect as other rights in the Bill of Rights, the
Court's decision reaffirmed that this right is integral to individual
liberty and cannot be relegated to "second-class" status.

Since that opinion came down in 2022, the *Bruen* decision has
had a seismic impact, shaking the foundations of restrictive gun laws
in states that had long held Second Amendment rights hostage to
arbitrary standards. Across the country, states with heavy-handed
gun regulations have found themselves on the defensive, facing a
wave of legal challenges rooted in the commonsense interpretation

that the right to bear arms is just that—a right, not a privilege to be selectively granted by the government.

In states like California and New York, the judiciary has already begun dismantling parts of their restrictive concealed-carry laws, forced at last to apply *Bruen*'s clear standard. Courts are no longer tolerating regimes that make law-abiding citizens jump through hoops simply to exercise a fundamental freedom. Instead, these cases are opening the door to restoring the Second Amendment as the framers intended—a check against the state, not a gift from it.

Over the past decade, something significant has changed in the legal battles over the Second Amendment. For years, both parties generally operated within the constitutional boundaries they believed the courts would uphold. But as progressives became more emboldened, they started using the courts not just to enforce existing laws but to push the Overton window—to redefine the very limits of what was acceptable under the Constitution. Rather than respecting precedent, they tried to stretch legal interpretations to fit their policy goals, often hoping activist judges would back them up. This strategy worked for a while, but with the rise of originalist judges and decisions like *Heller* and *Bruen*, the courts have started slapping these efforts down. More and more, the judiciary is restoring constitutional guardrails and making it clear that the Second Amendment, like all fundamental rights, is not up for reinterpretation based on political trends.

Advocates for gun rights, energized by the ruling, have ramped up their efforts, filing lawsuits that are finally putting antigun bureaucrats on notice: If you try to undermine this freedom, you will be challenged, and you will lose. And with each legal victory, the landscape shifts further toward restoring Americans' right to self-defense in all fifty states. The tide has turned, and the days of relegating the Second Amendment to second-class status are coming to an end.

But it hasn't happened without a significant fight, one of which happened right in my backyard.

Chapter 15

PROTECTING THE HOME

The crowd moved through the streets of St. Louis, chanting slogans and carrying signs. As they wound their way through the city, the protesters grew more agitated. Earlier, on the afternoon of June 28, 2020, they had announced plans to march to the home of St. Louis Mayor Lyda Krewson, who lived in the Central West End neighborhood. To get there, they entered Portland Place, a private, gated community.

The Black Lives Matter crowd had been harassing the white female mayor for days. I later learned she had to move out of her home for a period of time because of the threats and harassment. The mayor and I didn't agree on much, but we had gotten along personally, and these tactics were wrong. And on this particular day it seemed that the city was sitting on a powder keg. Since late May and early June of 2020, and the aftermath of George Floyd's death in Minneapolis, left-wing mobs had overrun our nation's major cities. They had burned down stores and set fire to cars. They had attacked police officers. In fact, in early June retired St. Louis Police Captain David Dorn was murdered by rioters as he was helping protect a friend's business.

During this time, the legacy media had declared that their riots were nothing but peaceful demonstrations. In one strange, downright Orwellian segment on CNN, an anchor stood on a street in front of burning buildings, describing with horror the scene that had just unfolded. The chyron beneath him read, "Fiery but mostly peaceful protests." Near the beginning of that summer, as tent cities were going up on the streets of her city, the mayor of Seattle had wondered if we were in for a "summer of love." It wasn't long before two people were killed by violent leftists in the tent city known as CHOP.

Watching the daylight protests turn into nighttime riots was the MO of the mobs in St. Louis, Kansas City, and nearly every urban center in America. People were frustrated but not many felt they could speak out. Worst of all, I knew that if these rioters damaged homes or hurt innocent people, they would probably get away with it. For a few years now, the city of St. Louis had lived under the regime of Kimberly Gardner, a left-wing prosecutor who had begun her term as the circuit attorney for St. Louis in January 2017.

In that time, Gardner had performed abysmally at her job. One of her first moves had been to announce that certain crimes would no longer be taken up by the Circuit Attorney's Office because prosecuting those crimes might lead to a lack of "equity" in the criminal justice system. She had no interest in even tackling violent crime. Looking back, we can see that these lazy, destructive policies were a harbinger of the psychosis that came over the left during the summer of 2020. These combined with the cultural Marxism and race essentialism pushed by the Left only further divided people. Anyone who tried to introduce any nuance, or suggested that we continue to prosecute violent crimes as they had always been prosecuted, was labeled a racist. This was a familiar theme that would permeate society during this timeframe. Once again, control the language and you have power, and that's what this was all about. It wasn't about truth or justice; it was about raw power and using race was a means to aggregate it.

That is why Gardner, as well as many other left-wing prosecutors, was allowed to do such damage in the years between 2017 and the present day. No one wanted to stand against them for fear that they would be socially ostracized for doing so. The same thing happened in Chicago, Los Angeles, and New York City, where far-left prosecutors effectively made crime legal for a few years, conducting a social experiment on millions of people that no one asked for. Or, more accurately, *almost* no one. It turns out that when you dig into the financing behind these rogue prosecutors, all roads lead back to the hedge fund billionaire George Soros. During the lead-up to the election of 2016, when everyone else was focused on the presidential race, Soros and his colleagues poured millions of dollars into tight local races, seeing the opportunity to infect the judicial system from the ground up.

In Philadelphia, for example, Soros poured $1.45 million into the race for district attorney, a staggering sum for a local election. This spending led to the election of Larry Krasner, a former defense attorney known for suing the police department multiple times. Once in office, Krasner immediately enacted policies that prioritized decriminalizing offenses over prosecuting them, weakening the consequences for a wide range of crimes. The effects were swift and devastating: Violent crime in Philadelphia surged, and neighborhoods once considered safe began to see spikes in shootings and other serious offenses. Soros's investment in Krasner paid off in reshaping Philadelphia's judicial system, but it was the residents who paid the ultimate price.

The same story repeated across the country. In San Francisco, Soros-backed funding helped elect Chesa Boudin as district attorney, a former public defender and the child of Weather Underground radicals. Boudin's policies went even further, aiming to dismantle what he called the "carceral state" by refusing to prosecute many misdemeanors and lowering charges on serious felonies. The result? A rapid rise in property crime and open-air drug markets, and a significant drop in arrests. Under Boudin, public safety eroded so drastically that San Francisco residents—many of whom initially supported progressive reforms—voted to recall him in 2022. He also backed Kim Gardner in St. Louis. These Soros-backed prosecutors turned entire cities into testing grounds for their ideological agendas, with consequences that ordinary people are still grappling with today.

The tide may be turning now, but we were still a long way away from that in the summer of 2020, when the mob was marching through the streets of St. Louis, headed for the mayor's home. But something happened on the way to the mayor's home that day: the McCloskeys.

If you watched the news during the summer of 2020, you can probably still remember the image of the McCloskeys that flew around the world in the aftermath of the protesters' march through the streets of St. Louis and outside their home. Mark McCloskey, dressed in khakis and a pink polo shirt, holds a rifle while standing outside his house. His wife holds a pistol. (They later made this image into a Christmas card.) They don't point these weapons at anyone. But they did stand outside their home defiantly. The protesters threatened to kill their dog and burn down their home as they stopped in front of the home. It was a tense moment. It was an image memorialized by legendary St. Louis photographer Bill Greenblatt, who has since passed away, that captured the essence of the tension that summer.

For the media, this was tantamount to assault or worse—the McCloskeys dared to stand up to the mob. It was also, somehow, racist, despite the fact that the mob running through the streets comprised people of all races and genders. This was predictable. During the "summer of love," there were at least three stories every day about people who had dared to stand against the mob, and in almost every case, those people's reputations were tarred and their motivations were called into question. When it came to ordinary citizens, the media's perspective was that no one could question anything, and if you did you were racist or should "check your privilege." Sadly, the liberal bias was on full display by outlets like CNN and MSNBC, both of which ran footage of the McCloskeys for days alongside headlines declaring them "gun-toting Karens."

So, what did the prosecutor of St. Louis city do? She never fully prosecuted the looters and the rioters; instead, she decided to prosecute . . . the McCloskeys. During this period of time, many felt powerless to stand up to this kind of abuse because taking on a black, female prosecutor was prima facia evidence you were a racist. Wrong. I decided to take on Kim Gardner, whose office had taken the extreme (and seriously stupid) step of filing charges against the McCloskeys for "unlawful use of a weapon," a felony under Missouri law. I didn't have to hear anything else before I knew we had to do something. Over the next few days, I was disgusted to see that Kim Gardner's office was using her spat with the McCloskeys in fundraising emails to her supporters. Shortly after those emails went out, my office took the decisive (and almost unprecedented) step of filing a brief urging the court to dismiss the charges, arguing that Gardner's move represented both prosecutorial overreach and also potential conflicts of interest.

More than anything else, I wanted to signal to the people of Missouri that they would not be punished for peacefully exercising their rights. This was a private street. The protesters were trespassing. Under Missouri law, the McCloskeys had every right to walk out onto their porch with guns in hand ready to defend their "castle." I firmly believed that if you saw prosecutors prosecuting lawful behavior like this, there would be a chilling effect on people exercising the constitutional right to self-defense. That is to say nothing of the overt hypocrisy of prosecuting this and not violent crime in the streets. I believed Gardner was abusing her authority and sending a message. That's why I took the unusual step of filing that brief as the people's lawyer. This was incredibly important at the time, given how lax many in government had been about enforcing the law against looters and rioters.

Besides, this wasn't my first rodeo with Kim Gardner's office.

*

When I first became Attorney General of Missouri, the world was different. It was January 2019, and the world didn't yet know terms such as *Covid-19* or *social distancing*. We hadn't yet experienced the Biden-Harris Administration's excesses. In my mind, one of the core missions of the office was fighting crime. For a few months, I had watched Kim Gardner, who had floated into office on a tide of Soros money, fail to do this. She had already begun to let the office go. Many felony cases weren't being prosecuted. Rather than prioritizing the prosecution of violent criminals, Gardner focused on social justice policies that satisfied her left-wing base. She championed efforts to eliminate cash bail for a broad range of offenders, ensuring that more criminals—including repeat offenders and those charged with serious crimes—were quickly released back onto the streets. The world needs social workers, but each jurisdiction only gets one prosecutor—someone responsible for making charging decisions against those who terrorize their fellow citizens. St. Louis, like many cities across America, had lost the security of knowing criminals would be held accountable because their prosecutor was more focused on ideology than on public safety. In Gardner's mind, the perpetrators were often seen as victims, while the actual victims were lower on the priority list. This is the damage the woke mind virus can cause.

So, very early in my tenure as Attorney General I met with Gardner at her office to see if she would be willing to let me prosecute some violent felonies that had been piling up in her office. While the Missouri Attorney General doesn't have original jurisdiction over local crimes, we can be asked to help. It happens a lot in rural counties where they may not have the resources or expertise to prosecute a double homicide, for example. The metros were different. In fact, prosecutors for a long time wanted to prosecute crime in cities because, sadly, they were able to do a lot of it. The same was true for cops who wanted to tackle real crime. But under the Gardner administration, experienced prosecutors and cops left in droves. This was a death spiral. Our office even picked up some of the prosecutors that left her office. So, I made the offer to Gardner to help. She never voluntarily did so. But I wasn't going to take no for an answer—too many lives and economic trajectory of my home region were at stake.

So, we decided to take action, doing the work that the circuit attorney was refusing to do. Plus, my team had former federal prosecutors Cris Stevens, whom I recruited to be my criminal chief, and Tom Albus, whom I recruited as well to be my First Assistant Attorney General, key positions and with important relationships. Working closely with the Trump-appointed United States Attorney Jeff Jensen, my office launched the Safer Streets Initiative, a first-of-its-kind program dedicated to fighting crime and picking up the slack that left-wing prosecutors simply couldn't and wouldn't handle. The idea came out of a meeting with Jeff, a tough, respected figure and a friend. With violent crime rates soaring in St. Louis and Kansas City and local prosecutors unwilling to act—particularly Kim Gardner—we found a way to work around them. Jeff had already doubled federal illegal gun prosecutions in St. Louis between 2017 and 2018, aiming to curb violence involving firearms by using federal resources to prosecute offenders more effectively. Our Safer Streets Initiative, which began in early 2019, deputized lawyers from my office as assistant US attorneys adding bandwidth for federal prosecutions. In August 2020, St. Louis and Kansas City had joined Operation Legend, a national federal intervention that brought over fifty federal agents to the city to support local law enforcement, resulting in hundreds of arrests and charges. The program, which was named after an African American child killed by gunfire during the riots that tore apart our cities that summer, stands as one of the most effective responses by the federal government to street-level violence. In the end, our Safer Streets Initiative filed nearly one thousand charges and secured hundreds of convictions. Sadly, the Biden Administration pulled the plug on this successful crime-fighting effort over petty politics.

We also took on the backlog of untested sexual assault kits. Early in my term, I learned that Missouri had nearly seven thousand untested sexual assault kits, just sitting there on shelves while the victims waited for answers. With the help of former Judge M. Keithley Williams, we led the nation in addressing this backlog through the SAFE Kit Initiative. Over $4.8 million in federal and state funds helped inventory, test, and process these kits, cutting the backlog by 93 percent and leading to hundreds of DNA matches, several convictions, and warrants. To bring justice to the families of victims in unsolved cases, we launched a Cold Case Unit with legendary St. Louis prosecutors Tom Dittmeier and Dean Hoag. This team, bolstered by advances in forensic science, continues to reexamine unresolved violent crimes.

Near the end of my first year in office, I got an opportunity to do the work that Kim Gardner's office wouldn't do in an unusual way. In 2020, the case of a man named Antonio Muldrew was set to go to trial in St. Louis. Gardner's office could not handle the case due to a conflict of interest; one of her former assistants had previously represented Muldrew, who had allegedly shot a convenience store clerk during a robbery, so we got the case. I decided that I wanted to help prosecute the case myself. I felt it was important to send a message to the people of St. Louis that I was willing to roll up my sleeves and do the work myself. The people of St. Louis deserved to live in safe communities, and victims deserved justice, and they had an Attorney General who would fight for them. I dug it. As I prepared, I learned quickly that Muldrew was guilty as hell, and I was determined to put him away. The stakes were even higher given the fact that I, a sitting Attorney General, was helping prosecute the case in St. Louis—that had never been done before. This was, indeed, a rare move, and the criminal jury pools in the city can be challenging. I knew if I was going to do this I had to win.

The trial began on January 6, 2020. As the people of Missouri watched, we laid out every horrifying detail of the case. We presented overwhelming evidence, including forensic evidence and DNA from a cigarette butt Muldrew had left at the scene.

In my opening statement to the jury, I began by quoting Clint Eastwood, who played Missouri outlaw, turned farmer, turned vigilante William Munny in the 1992 classic *Unforgiven*, "It's a hell of a thing, killin' a man. You take away all he's got and all he's ever gonna have." I then explained to the jury how Muldrew had gunned down Abdulrauf Kadir, an Ethiopian refugee working two jobs to support his family in a Kenyan refugee camp. Kadir wanted to bring his family to America and was saving up to do that. Kadir had pleaded for his life, telling Muldrew about his wife and two children. But Muldrew, intent on getting what he wanted, ignored him, emptied the register, stole a 9mm pistol, and shot Kadir twice in the head as he lay on the floor.

This trial wasn't just about one man's crime; it was about justice for Kadir and his family, and accountability in a city where the criminal justice system had been failing victims. When the jury handed down the life sentence without parole, it was a moment of vindication—not just for Kadir's family but for every law-abiding citizen of St. Louis who had grown tired of a system that too often allowed violent criminals to walk free.

That's the difference between my approach to justice and the approach of people like Kim Gardner. They lose sight of who the real victims are. Ironically, the "social justice" crusaders miss one really big thing—individual justice. They look at the system and see numbers—percentages, statistics—and decide their goal is to lower incarceration rates, no matter the cost. But conservatives look at the system and see people. We see the victims, like Kadir, who are too often forgotten in the rush to make excuses for criminals. The truth is too many families are being torn apart by violence that goes unpunished. Justice means standing up for those victims and making sure their day in court matters. It means standing up to the bullies on the bus and being a last line of defense.

The prosecution and verdict also sent a message to citizens that they didn't have to live under a regime that excused criminals and failed to prosecute crimes. Just because George Soros wanted to spend billions of dollars to tear down the United States didn't mean we all had to be okay with it. Later that year, as the world seemed to turn to chaos in the streets, as I prepared to file my motion to have Kim Gardner's charges against the McCloskeys dismissed, I couldn't help but think about this. Sometimes, sending a message to people to show that someone is actually fighting for them inspires hope even in the darkest time. That spark, that light in the darkness, became a beacon guiding our way. We see it clearer now, but back then it was important to hold that candle in the darkness—particularly during that harrowing summer of 2020 when footage of burning buildings led the news every evening.

The response was about what I had expected. On the Left, I was lambasted as a supporter of armed resistance to peaceful protest. Of course, nothing could be further from the truth. In fact, I filed the brief so quickly because I knew just how important it was to stand up for the rights of American citizens, especially when doing so would be seen as unpopular by many. Also, the law was once again on my side. In the state of Missouri, we have something known as the Castle Doctrine, which states that individuals have the right to use force, including deadly force, to protect themselves from intruders in their homes, vehicles, or any place they have a legal right to be. This law removes the obligation to retreat, allowing individuals to stand their ground. Under Missouri Revised Statutes § 563.031, a person may use physical force if they reasonably believe it is necessary to defend themselves or others from imminent unlawful force. Deadly force is justified if they believe it is necessary to prevent death, serious physical injury, or any forcible felony.

Given the circumstances on the ground, this law seemed to apply. In my brief for dismissal, I wrote:

> *The right to use firearms to defend one's person, family, home, and property has deep roots in Missouri law. Self-defense is the central component of the right to keep and bear arms, which receives the highest level of protection from the Missouri Constitution. Missouri's statutes specifically authorize Missouri citizens to use firearms to deter assailants and protect themselves, their families, and homes from threatening or violent intruders. A highly publicized criminal prosecution of Missouri citizens for exercising these fundamental freedoms threatens to intimidate and deter law-abiding Missouri citizens from exercising their constitutional right of self-defense. . . . On behalf of all Missourians who wish to exercise their right to keep and bear arms in self-defense of their persons, homes, families, and property, the Attorney General respectfully requests that the Court dismiss this case at the earliest possible opportunity.*

Luckily, I wasn't the only one willing to stand behind the McCloskeys. On August 3, 2021, after the McCloskeys had entered into a plea deal, Governor Mike Parson pardoned Mark and Patricia McCloskey, saying, "We stand by individuals' rights under the Castle Doctrine and will not allow law-abiding citizens to be made into criminals for exercising their right to protect their home."

It's no surprise that Mark McCloskey became a popular figure around Missouri. He took the fame he had gained on that afternoon in the summer of 2020 and later mounted a campaign for the United States Senate in 2022. The field was crowded that campaign season. It included nearly two dozen other Republicans, including me. Fortunately, things never got ugly between me and Mark. And since then, we've remained friendly. He ran as a political outsider, and I don't blame Mark for trying it out. I'm sure he doesn't blame me for praising him on the campaign trail at every opportunity, a move that I also knew would throw cold water on any criticisms he might have of me.

For Kim Gardner, things didn't go so well. In the aftermath of the unrest we saw during the summer of 2020, pressure mounted on her to resign, and it wasn't only because she had failed to prosecute serious crimes. The court system publicly expressed alarm over the growing backlog of "hundreds of serious cases on the trial docket." There was also incredibly high staff turnover in her office, given that she was incredibly difficult to work for, and a few other scandals. In the end, it was one tragic and highly publicized case that broke the dam. On February 18, 2023, a man named Daniel Riley crashed into Janae Edmondson, a seventeen-year-old volleyball player from Tennessee who was in St. Louis for a tournament, causing her to lose both her legs. Riley had been arrested over fifty times for various violations, but thanks to policies pushed by Gardner and other Democrats, he had walked free again and again.

The fallout from Edmondson's case was swift. Public outcry over Gardner's failure to act reached a fever pitch, with citizens, local leaders, and the state government officials calling for her immediate resignation. My successor Andrew Bailey rightly began to seek her ouster from office. It was about this case but so much more—it was how her office had become, as a St. Louis City judge described it, a "rudderless ship of chaos." In May 2023, under mounting legal and political pressure, Gardner stepped down, marking the end of a complete disaster for the people of Missouri. (Gardner continues to claim this was all politically motivated.) Her departure hopefully signaled a turning point for St. Louis, a chance to rebuild a justice system that had long neglected the very people it was meant to protect. Today, our governor Mike Kehoe is working with my successor Andrew Bailey, who was instrumental in the fight against Gardner, to make public safety a priority. And with Donald Trump back in the White House, we can fully expect a return to law and order and maybe even more cooperative efforts like our Safer Streets program to tackle violent crime. I know I'll be helping any way I can, including working with federal law enforcement to make our communities safer.

Part VI

Fighting Woke

Chapter 16

CRT, DEI, AND WHEN
PARENTS WERE THE ENEMY

During Covid, every day brought a new story about some insane thing that had occurred in a classroom. Some of these stories were shared on social media by concerned parents who were confused, alarmed, and angry about what was going on in our educational system. One parent in Washington posted on Facebook about a survey that had been given to her young child about gender and sexual preferences. Another parent found homework in her child's backpack that made reference to "nonmonogamous relationships."

Other things took a little more digging. After realizing that something was very wrong in our schools—and that something *had* been wrong for quite some time—various organizations turned to the tools of investigative journalism to uncover what was going on. One of these organizations was headed by a former documentary filmmaker named Christopher Rufo, who had spent his career uncovering wrongdoing at various public institutions. Beginning in early 2020, Rufo refocused his career on uncovering the sudden profusion of woke ideology in our schools. It began in his hometown of Seattle, where he realized that teachers were being trained on a document that asked them to "examine their privilege" and treat students of color differently than white students. He created a tip line for parents to report what they were seeing in schools.

The results were downright insane. In a school in upstate New

York, we learned, children were shown a video that described the United States as a "white supremacist regime." Kids in fifth grade were shown cartoons that described a "school-to-grave pipeline" for black men, which was narrated by the ghosts of unarmed black people who had been killed by police—something that the radical Left has assured us for years happens every single day in the United States.

As the dad of school-aged kids, I felt compelled to find out more. I wanted to know like other parents, was this nonsense happening in schools here in Missouri, to children and families I'd been elected to represent? If it was, I wanted to do something about it. I knew the education establishment would be against me, and they were, but I didn't care. Luckily, the Attorney General's Office already had an open line of communication set up for parents. We hadn't shut it down just because the mask and vaccine mandates had ended. As the reports of strange woke lessons came pouring in, I decided to put another call out to parents and students. If your teachers or school administrators were trying to push woke nonsense down your throat, I wanted to know about it. And I wanted to take action. Over the next few months, we would get reports that were shocking and strange. The things that our children were being taught sounded like the weirdest game of woke Mad Libs you'd ever played.

One parent submitted a screenshot of a homework assignment that asked her child to analyze a novel through the lens of Marxism and gender identity.[1] Another told the horrifying story of a child who had been forced to do a "privilege walk," taking steps forward in front of his classmates because of his white skin and the neighborhood he'd grown up in.[2] We learned that students were being assigned full chapters from textbooks that were written by left-wing activists, and that they had access to borderline pornographic books in school libraries.

The message from the schools was clear. School bureaucrats

believed that *they* were in charge of our children while they were in school, and anyone who attempted to fight back would be socially ostracized.

Or worse.

*

For a long time, the warped lessons that were being taught in our schools were hidden from parents. As soon as we found out, there were few ways to vent our frustrations. One outlet was school board meetings, which gave parents all over the country opportunities to demand answers about what their children were being taught. In the aftermath of Covid-19, when some of the most absurd lessons about wokeness and gender ideology were revealed, some of these school board meetings grew heated—and with good reason.

Parents gave speeches denouncing the school system, which had adopted nonsensical texts such as the *1619 Project* in classrooms, spreading the vicious (and thoroughly debunked) lie that the United States was founded to preserve slavery. Speaking about critical race theory during a school board meeting, a black father earned uproarious applause by saying, "When you talk about critical race theory, which is pretty much when we're telling kids how to *hate* each other, dislike each other. That's what it comes down to. You're going to deliberately teach kids these black kids got it better than them because they're white? You're going to tell a white kid, 'oh the black people are all down and oppressed?' How do I have two medical degrees if I'm sitting here oppressed?"[3]

Naturally, the powers that be were not pleased at being questioned in this way. Throughout the school year, parents were faced with short time limits for speakers, canceled meetings, and sudden changes in policy that took away the right for parents to speak. Sometimes the administrators didn't bother to show up at all. These blatant acts of disrespect piled up, and parents grew furious, as they should have. There were some meetings, such as the ones held in Loudoun County, Virginia, during the fall of 2021, where the crowds who'd come to speak were deliberately lied to.

During one such meeting on June 22, 2021, an administrator addressed the question of a controversial new policy that would allow children who said they were trans to use restrooms meant for the opposite gender. Speaking to the audience in a condescending tone, he said, "*Time* magazine in 2016 called that a red herring, that the data was simply not playing out that transgender students were more likely to assault cisgender students in restrooms than were other students. . . . I think it's important to keep our perspective on this, we've heard it several times tonight from our public speakers but the predator transgender student or person simply does not exist."

The problem, of course, was that this phenomenon was very real. It had happened to one of the people sitting in the audience, who had been waiting for his turn to speak when he found out that the public-comment section of the meeting had been canceled. The man's name was Scott Smith, and he'd been in the middle of a nightmare for months. In May of that year, his daughter had been brutally assaulted in a school bathroom by a boy wearing a dress—who, if the policy up for debate that evening went through, would be more than welcome to use the girls' bathroom. Rather than punishing the student or reporting him to the police, however, the school had covered up for him, arranging for a quiet transfer to another school. When Smith went to the school to demand answers, the school principal called the police on him and claimed he was being hysterical.

I can only imagine the frustration he felt. First, he was denied the right to speak. Then, as he sat there listening to the school board members belittle the concerns of parents, one of the members of the school board insisted that the very thing that had happened to his daughter never, in fact, happened to anyone. According to Luke

Rosiak, who broke this horrific story for *The Daily Wire*, the meeting quickly devolved into chaos when a woman sitting next to Smith began harassing him. The two exchanged words, and Smith raised his voice. A few seconds later, he found himself thrown to the ground by a police officer who had been stationed at the back of the room. His shirt flew up over his stomach, and people took pictures.

Within hours, the photograph of Smith being wrestled to the ground was all over the world. It led news broadcasts, and it showed up on the homepages of dozens of left-wing websites. Not since the image of the McCloskeys defending their home had the Left's ire been so focused on one person. To the liberal media, Smith represented *a clear and present danger to the school system*. He was, as one reporter at Buzz-Feed News incorrectly put it, an "angry white parent" who wanted to "use violence" against the school board. Almost no one bothered to dig in and learn the real story. When Rosiak at *The Daily Wire* did, he learned that the student who had assaulted Smith's daughter—the one who was allowed to wear dresses and use the women's room despite being a dangerous biological male—went on to sexually assault *another* girl at the school to which he was quietly transferred.

In September 2021, the National School Boards Association (NSBA) sent a letter to Attorney General Merrick Garland, complaining about a supposed "uptick in violence and intimidation" against school officials, citing incidents like the Scott Smith case as evidence. The letter detailed additional instances of alleged threats and harassment, though many did not involve actual violence. In response, on October 4, 2021, Attorney General Garland issued a memorandum to the FBI and U.S. Attorneys' Offices directing them to address the reported threats against school administrators, board members, teachers, and staff. The memo emphasized the need to protect public servants from illegal threats and intimidation.

Buried in the text of the original letter from the NSBA was a shocking suggestion that the Biden Justice Department use provisions of the PATRIOT Act to go after parents who simply showed up at school board meetings to voice their concerns. Most Americans understand the PATRIOT Act as a tool to combat terrorism. But by invoking it here, the NSBA and the Biden administration were unmistakably drawing a line in the sand. Parents who dared to speak out against left-wing educational agendas were now branded as "domestic terrorists." The incident that triggered this letter, involving Scott Smith—a father who was tackled and arrested just for standing up for his brutalized daughter at a school board meeting—was used to justify this attack on parental rights. It's clear this was about sending a message to every concerned parent in America: If you question the woke agenda, you're a target. The Biden Justice Department, under Garland's leadership, responded swiftly to this declaration of war on parents, proving that their priority wasn't public safety—it was silencing dissent.

Even more troubling, the timing of the letter in the fall of 2021 appeared to be calculated to influence the outcome of the 2021 election for Virginia governor. Education had become a hot topic that was hurting the Democratic candidate, Terry McAuliffe, and the anger of parents at school board meetings in Virginia was a focal point of voters' dissatisfaction with failed Democratic educational policies. By threatening parents' First Amendment–protected speech, Biden's Justice Department appeared to be engaged in a transparent, deliberate election attempt at interference—an egregious practice that would reach even greater heights with the prosecutions of President Trump two years later.

Once again, we were seeing the Left's playbook in action. A few concerned parents would have been something that the Left had to take seriously. But *domestic terrorists* who wanted to commit violent acts and intimidate members of school boards was an Emergency™, and it would allow the Left to use all the tools at their disposal to fight back. That meant the FBI, which was put on notice in Garland's memo, would be weaponized. It meant intimidation and censorship. It meant all the things they had been using to try to attack conservatives—most prominently Donald Trump himself—since Joe Biden took office.

It was the kind of thing that an enterprising investigative journalist might have been interested to report on. I'm sure that if Richard Nixon had done even one-tenth of this, *The Washington Post* would have been all over it. But by 2021, America's legacy media was little more than a mouthpiece for the Democratic Party. When Scott Smith was tackled at the school board meeting in Loudoun County, legacy media outlets didn't send anyone down to Virginia to figure out what happened. They just took the left-wing propaganda that he was a "domestic terrorist" at face value and printed it. If it weren't for Luke Rosiak at *The Daily Wire*, we might have never learned the full story.

While I appreciated the work that these independent journalists were doing, the legacy media was on board with this radical agenda and had real disdain for normal folks speaking out. You could almost hear them saying under their collective breath, "Check your privilege." But I wanted to know more. Every day, we had ridiculous stories pouring into our parent portal in Missouri. But I wondered what else was out there. How many strange lessons were being taught to our kids that no one was speaking out about? Given what had happened to Scott Smith, I had a feeling that the number of parents willing to go to school board meetings and demand answers was going to shrink every day. Ordinary citizens really didn't want to become the "main character" of left-wing Twitter to take a stand in public. They had jobs they didn't want to lose and reputations that they didn't want to have dragged through the mud.

I, on the other hand, already had plenty of battle scars and was unafraid. There wasn't much left that the mob could do to me. So, I had my team keep digging. One of the most important tools we used to do this was the Freedom of Information Act, known as FOIA, or in Missouri, the Sunshine Law. For decades this act had been a go-to method for journalists to uncover things that the government wanted to keep hidden. During Republican administrations, they used it all the time. Under Joe Biden, whose interests they wanted to protect, not so much. Luckily, anyone could file FOIA requests to get information out of the government. The key was knowing how to format those requests and word them correctly so that the bureaucrat in charge of responding didn't get to stonewall you. In Missouri, the Sunshine Law was often used pretty selectively against Republicans, although not exclusively. There were some legitimate journalists doing good work to expose corruption, but by and large this was a tool used against Republicans. My office was actually tasked with enforcing Sunshine Law violations, and we had done more on that front than my predecessors. But what the Left never saw coming was my desire to use it to expose bias and what was really happening in our schools. I would do the work journalists avoided because these school districts were preferred institutions now for those who shared this ideology. So we got to work.

The results were unreal. One of the things we uncovered was a presentation given by a person named Yvania Garcia-Pusateri, the chief equity and diversity officer of the largest school district in the state—Springfield Public Schools. Alongside her during this presentation was *another* manager of diversity, equity, and inclusion who, on his LinkedIn page, advertised counseling services for "all couples needing relationship help, including open/non-monogamous/poly-amorous couples," "individuals questioning/exploring their sense of gender and sexuality," and "ethnic, religious, and other minorities." The presentation, according to Parents Defending Education, included discussion of "gender unicorn relationships." The explanation in the presentation—which, again, was given to people in charge of educating the children of Springfield, Missouri, read:

You may recognize this graphic as similar to The Genderbread Person. We created this graphic with significant changes to more accurately portray the distinction between gender, sex assigned at birth, and sexuality. Ultimately, we wanted to recognize genders outside of the western gender binary, which the Genderbread Person does not. Not all trans people exist on a scale of womanhood and manhood. There are several other issues with this graphic such as the use of the inaccurate term "biological sex," the use of "asex" (which fails to recognize that everyone has sex characteristics prescribed to them), and several other issues with terminology and presentation.

In other documents, teachers were informed about the "Oppression Matrix," and a "Pyramid of White Supremacy," both explicitly Marxist documents that made the case that all white children were somehow complicit in white supremacy. We learned that kids were being forced to participate in "privilege walks," during which students were ranked according to how much white privilege they have, later being made to apologize for it. Clearly, this nonsense was everywhere. It wasn't just St. Louis and Kansas City; this was Springfield. They got on our radar because they had threatened to charge citizens, and then a state representative, tens of thousands of dollars to disclose and produce these documents. They couldn't do that, but it took us to come in and get them. On top of their subterfuge was the fact that this stuff had made it into our schools—which was remarkable. But it was even *more* remarkable that the school system had been able to hide it for so long.

An often-heard refrain was "Critical Race Theory (CRT) isn't a course." This of course disguised the fact that if they are training administrators, teachers, and staff to divide the classroom by race, then every class is infected with this divisive ideology rooted in cultural Marxism.

Between the information from our Sunshine Law requests and

the stories that were coming in every day through our parent portal, my office had a wealth of insane information that we felt needed to be shared with the world. I did this through speeches, news conferences, and daily tweets from my official account. As I did so, I noticed that the need to protect our kids was turning even nonpolitical people into activists. Parents were waking up. I was invited to an event organized by Moms for Liberty. The group was a collection of mothers who wanted to learn how they could make an impact on their local communities through politics. After speaking with them for a few minutes, I learned that only three of the ninety or so women in attendance had ever been to a political event before. The other eighty-seven had come out because they'd been spurred to action by the material that was being taught in schools.

Near the end of the event, one of the mothers approached me and said she was a teacher. Unlike some of the other people in attendance, she knew just how bad things were getting at our schools, and she'd known it for a long time. Not long after I spoke to the group, she quit her job and wanted to come work for my Senate campaign. She was hired and did great work. So did dozens of other volunteers, many of whom had been inspired to get into politics because they'd become fed up with being viewed by the Biden Administration as "domestic terrorists" just because they wanted to have a say in what their children were learning. Throughout my campaign, real energy came from these parents. They showed up in groups of five, ten, and twenty, packing the house at lots of speeches I gave. Clearly, something was resonating. Parents knew I was fighting for them and their kids, and that tapped into something very powerful—the kind of thing that allows you to ultimately win in a landslide in a twenty-one-person primary, and later in a general election when you are massively outspent.

I campaigned all over Missouri and the disclosures kept coming. Parent-portal messages continued to roll in as people realized that they wouldn't have their lives ruined just for speaking out. As with most things, there was strength in numbers. What started with a few concerned parents became a movement that even the federal government couldn't suppress. All over the country, school boards began changing over. Parents got angry. The tide was turning. I issued subpoenas to school districts demanding documents and information on invasive student surveys given to kids about race, gender, sexuality, and political ideology without parental consent. My office also pushed back against Biden's Department of Education when they proposed a rule that would have given schools that taught divisive CRT preferential treatment in grant applications. We did this by partnering with nineteen other states to write a letter to the Department of Education, knowing that we had the support of the people.

"Though the Department does not overtly refer to CRT (Critical Race Theory) in its priorities," we wrote, "it is prioritizing teaching this highly controversial ideology through the vehicle of this grant program. This is hardly what Congress intended when it authorized this program. CRT focuses how our current government mechanisms are irretrievably flawed. Its theorists posit that our Nation's values, ideals, foundations and institutions—the things Congress intended to promote—instead produce 'inequity' demanding actions to modify this result. This appears to be a view shared by Professor Ibram X. Kendi and advanced through the 1619 Project. It is fair to assume this view would be advanced by a curriculum built from its project."

In the end, the Biden Department of Education backed down, sensing that the tide was finally turning against them. We won, and we won because we were willing to fight back. Shortly thereafter, I won my campaign for the United States Senate, an enormous victory not just for me but for all the people who had stood with me during this important fight. We saw a similar result in Virginia, the place where the Scott Smith incident had happened, where Republican Glenn Youngkin defeated Democrat Terry McAuliffe to become governor. The final nail in McAuliffe's coffin had come during a debate, when he said, "I don't think parents should be telling schools what they should teach."

Since then, we've seen school boards shift to look more like the communities they serve. Parents who were politically awakened during the lockdowns have gotten involved and made a serious difference in what our children are being taught. It is no longer mandatory for teachers to tell kids that the United States of America was founded on the principle of white supremacy, or to make them do "privilege walks" and apologize for slavery. But the fight isn't over. As we saw in the *New York Times* story at the beginning of this chapter, too many folks in teachers' unions and school administrators still believe that parents are the enemy. Radical gender ideology and CRT have not gone away, just maybe a bit more underground. And now that President Trump is back in the White House, we are sure to see a resurgence of "The Resistance."

Fortunately, we've developed our own playbook over the years, and we know exactly how to fight back.

Chapter 17

TAKING ON THE CLIMATE ALARMISTS, ESG, AND THE NET-ZERO BANKING ALLIANCE

When I was growing up in my working-class neighborhood in the shadow of St. Louis Lambert International Airport with TWA planes landing nearly overhead, Democrats often attempted to land a familiar line of attack against Republicans. They would claim that Republicans were nothing more than shills for corporate America, handing out tax breaks for the rich and taking care of their wealthy friends at the expense of working people. I argued, even back then, that this wasn't true, but it most certainly isn't true with the political realignment ushered in by President Donald Trump.

Anyone who doubts this need only take a look at some of the footage from late in the 2024 campaign cycle, when President Trump was packing arenas with working-class folks in cities all over the country while Kamala Harris was sticking mostly to her rich friends and Hollywood elites. I was there with him; I saw the folks lined up for a glimpse of him and his America First message. In the closing days of the campaign, I would fire up arenas holding thirty thousand patriots ready to hear him speak. These folks would wait for hours. Tens of thousands of others were outside hoping to get in. Even more lined the streets on the way into the arenas. We've never seen anything like this phenomenon. He has been a vessel for those who felt the system was working against them, and in the end, they just wanted a better life for their families. They were called "deplorables" or "garbage" for it. That was like adding rocket fuel to the movement and the transformation of the GOP into the multiethnic working-class party it is today.

Looking back from a purely political lens, I find it kind of amazing that it took this long for the old paradigm to break down. It has been obvious for a long time that Democrats do not care about working people. Among voters without a college degree, Trump secured 57 percent of the vote, while Harris received just 41 percent. On the flip side, among college graduates, Harris led with 60 percent, compared to Trump's 39 percent. These numbers reveal a growing educational divide, one that underscores the transformation of the Republican Party into the voice of America's working class.

This is true everywhere in the country. But it's even more prevalent in Missouri, where I've spent virtually my whole life. During my childhood, almost all my friends' parents were factory workers, truck drivers, small business owners, cops—blue-collar folks. They were the backbone of our community and, now, of this movement. In the 1980s, the Democrat Party was still identified as the party "for the little guy," as my grandfather on my mom's side would say. He was a union forklift operator and thought that Republicans were out for the rich. Because of my dad's populist streak, I always believed differently. In my early years I would watch CNN's *Crossfire* with my dad in the living room. He worked seven days a week and the midnight shift so he'd be home in the early evenings to watch my games, to be there for dinner and for some TV watching in the days when you really only had one TV in the house. I'd watch people like Jack Kemp and Pat Buchanan thunder away speaking up for regular folks, and they were Republicans. I also remember a few arguments of my own with my friends' parents, during which I would make the case, Don't you and I know better how to spend our money than the government? And they'd tell me I didn't understand. But I knew this was a winning argument. Reagan's presidency started to challenge the assumptions of the two parties, but the Democrats hadn't gone off the deep end yet and the central political figure of our time, Donald J. Trump, wasn't yet on the political stage.

Under President Trump's leadership, the Republican Party was pulled toward working-class policies for the first time in many years, often against the advice of the supposed "experts" at the Republican National Committee. Suddenly a working-class coalition emerged—composed of blue-collar workers, small business owners, farmers, and families from the heartland who had long felt overlooked by the political elite. This new coalition wasn't bound exclusively by traditional conservative priorities alone, but by a shared sense of cultural pride, economic empowerment, and a deep distrust of the establishment. In 2024, President Trump made gains in nearly every demographic in the country, especially with younger voters. Among Latino voters, his support increased from 38 percent in 2020 to over 44 percent in 2024; driven by concerns about the economy and cultural alignment, Trump increased his vote share in urban and working-class communities in 2024. Trump also strengthened his standing among male voters, including black men and particularly white working-class men, increasing his share from 55 percent in 2020 to 60 percent in 2024. Regionally, Trump made significant gains in urban areas, including heavily Latino and immigrant neighborhoods in cities like New York, where concerns about crime and economic challenges resonated with voters. In the Northeast, traditionally a Democratic stronghold, he expanded his reach in states like New York and Pennsylvania, signaling a growing appeal to voters disenchanted with progressive policies.

Trump's message resonated particularly with those who had watched their communities decline due to decades of offshoring, globalist policies, and disregard from both parties. His America

First platform gave a voice to those who had been left behind by the twin horsemen of globalism: bad trade deals and unprotected borders. Trump spoke to prioritizing *American* jobs and industry. Unlike the Republicans before him, who focused on corporate tax cuts and financial markets, Trump's policies spoke to the everyday concerns of working Americans, challenging the influence of big business interests over the party. Meanwhile, the Democratic Party, traditionally the party of the working class, had transformed, becoming the preferred party of large corporations, ultra-woke elites, Silicon Valley tech giants, and Wall Street—a shift marked by their strong alignment with globalism and progressive social issues that often alienated Middle America.

The 2024 election results proved that this coalition was not only durable but decisive. Trump's victory represented a resounding mandate for this realigned Republican Party, cementing its identity as the party of working Americans. The Democratic Party, now firmly entrenched as the party of cultural elites, found itself struggling to connect with the very voters it once claimed to champion. This unprecedented realignment left the Democrats with an identity crisis, while the Republicans, driven by the priorities of everyday Americans, secured a powerful foothold in modern American politics.

Although it was the 2024 election results that revealed this to the world—and to the liberal legacy media, which has always been slow to catch up—it was evident long before Kamala Harris and Tim Walz lost in a landslide to President Trump, despite outspending him by tens of millions of dollars. As far back as 2019, when I was just getting used to my new position as the AG of Missouri, we saw signs that even big business was going seriously woke. Rather than just the Hollywood elite, the radical Left seemed to have captured the corporate elite as well. The CEOs of big banks were suddenly speaking out on woke social issues; companies hired more diversity, equity, and inclusion (DEI) officers than ever, bringing people like

Robin DiAngelo (author of *White Fragility*) in to give mandatory white-guilt seminars.

According to an account of one person who was forced to endure a corporate struggle session at the Coca-Cola Company in 2021, participants were told to "try to be less white," by which the seminar leader meant "less arrogant, less certain, and less oppressive." Such nonsense would not have been possible in a corporate setting before roughly 2014 or so, when big social media companies gave woke leftists the power to cancel anyone who disagreed with them. As we saw in the chapter on *Missouri v. Biden*, these Big Tech companies exerted enormous influence on our national conversation, piping woke orthodoxy out to the world and pretending it was normal. At the time, Big Tech companies had employee bases that contributed almost exclusively to Democrats. They silenced the views of conservatives, tricking employees of major corporations into believing that "woke" was the new order of the day.

But it wasn't only American companies. There was also pressure from activist organizations. In April 2023, the *New York Post* reported on the existence of something known as the "Corporate Equity Index," or "CEI," a score given to American companies every year by a group called Human Rights Campaign. According to the *Post*, the group,

> which has received millions from George Soros' Open Society Foundation among others, issues report cards for America's biggest corporations via the CEI: awarding or subtracting points for how well companies adhere to what HRC calls its "rating criteria." ...
> The main categories are: "Workforce Protections," "Inclusive Benefits," "Supporting an Inclusive Culture," "Corporate Social Responsibility and Responsible Citizenship." A company can lose CEI points if it doesn't fulfill HRC's demand for "integration of intersectionality in professional development, skills-based or other

training" or if it doesn't use a "supplier diversity program with demonstrated effort to include certified LGBTQ+ suppliers."

You might wonder why companies care so much about this score. The answer, of course, lies with a new movement that took hold in corporate America—particularly private equity companies—in the late 2010s. The movement is called ESG, which stands for "environmental, social, and governance," and it has radically changed the way business in America works. Rather than maximizing profits for shareholders, which is why corporations are supposed to exist in the first place, firms that prioritize ESG adhere to woke talking points, measuring their success in how well they are effecting the kind of change that left-wing activists want to see in the world. Private equity firms claim that they are able to do this *and* make money for the millions of Americans who are invested in them through their pensions and retirement accounts. They would certainly like us to believe they can do both.

In reality, though, ESG loses money. Although private equity firms and the companies that are forced to go woke to appease them pretend otherwise, left-wing causes are not good for anyone's bottom line. They just don't care because they can afford to take the hit—and they may fear the wrath of the Left and its media allies if they don't toe the line. But ordinary Americans can't afford to take this hit.

As I watched the ESG phenomenon unfold, I spoke often with other Republican Attorneys General about how we might be able to fight back. We all agreed that this takeover of corporate America presented a clear and present danger to consumers and ordinary investors. We knew that a cabal of global elites hijacking our capitalist system, coercing corporations, and threatening the hard-earned dollars of working Americans was going to put us in a bad place. One of the most troubling things we saw was the "Net-Zero

Alliance," which had been hanging over the heads of Americans for years.

In some sense, this began in 2017, shortly after President Trump had pulled the United States out of the Paris Climate Accords. Rather than complying—or staying out of politics altogether—many American business leaders decided to rebuke the President publicly, looking for ways to implement climate policy by going around the federal government. This wasn't just big business giving lip service to climate activism—it was an orchestrated takeover by the Left and their allies, leveraging these so-called crises. Take Climate Action 100+, for example. Launched in December 2017, it was one of the most brazen initiatives yet, assembled with the explicit goal of enforcing climate policy independently of government decision-making. The event was held in Paris to mark the second anniversary of the Paris Climate Accords. President Trump wasn't even invited to the summit, but who was there? Billionaires like Michael Bloomberg and Bill Gates, and private citizen John Kerry, representing the epitome of the Left's elite class—people who believe they are above our democratic process.

Fast-forward to the Biden Administration and these alliances only intensified. Biden entered office with razor-thin congressional control, which should have limited his ability to push forward extreme climate policies. But the elites backing him were prepared. They doubled down, expanding their own influence through initiatives like the Net-Zero Banking Alliance, launched in April 2021 with forty-three founding members. Banks in this alliance committed to steering their investments and loan portfolios away from the industries that sustained our economy, singling out coal, oil and gas, agriculture, and even residential real estate as targets, and starving those productive businesses of capital. Their goal? A radical agenda that required choking off industries they deemed undesirable, regardless of the real-world impact on jobs, families, and American competitiveness.

These Net-Zero and ESG alliances operated as stealth agents for the Left's agenda, targeting businesses with a combination of capital denial, internal shareholder mutinies, and intimidation tactics aimed at corporate boards. If a company refused to align with their woke demands, it faced blacklisting and potential destruction. Make no mistake—this was an assault on capitalism itself, a coordinated attack to impose an ideological agenda that no voter approved, and that no sane investor would endorse. The numbers didn't lie either: ESG funds continued to underperform the broader market, with returns falling more than 250 basis points below the average. For the millions of Americans whose retirement funds were tied up in these investments, this was nothing short of theft by mismanagement, putting woke ideology ahead of fiduciary duty.

Meanwhile, this Net-Zero zealotry drove up energy prices for everyone. With fossil fuels as their primary target, these alliances were shrinking America's energy output, making basic utilities more costly and hitting lower-income families hardest. Energy costs were regressive, and as these costs climbed, it was the working class—those least able to shoulder this burden—who suffered the most.

It was exactly the kind of thing that we believed we could use the legal system to fight against. However, we understood that this was a giant problem. Unlike some of our other fights, it wasn't just one entity, or one group of entities, engaging in this kind of malfeasance. It was hundreds of people and dozens of elite institutions, all doing hundreds of different bad things in hundreds of slightly different ways. So we strategized, working together to put holes in the armor of firms that were bankrupting Americans through their ESG practices.

The list of our accomplishments on this front is long. While Joe Biden was in office, Republican AGs worked together to, among other things, launch investigations into the Net-Zero Banking Alliance and its members—JPMorgan Chase, Goldman Sachs, Bank of America,

Citigroup, Wells Fargo, and Morgan Stanley—and Climate Action 100+, targeting global steering committee members like Franklin Templeton and the California Public Employees Retirement System, or CalPERS. Morningstar Investment Management also came under our scrutiny for its ESG-driven practices.

We didn't hold back in warning asset managers about the legal risks of ESG investments and putting ESG goals ahead of making money for their clients. We criticized the ESG influence of proxy firms like International Shareholder Services Inc. and Glass, Lewis & Co., and demanded that S&P stop including ESG credit indicators in state and local government ratings.

Throughout this period, we pushed back against numerous federal proposals attempting to embed ESG into the core of our financial system. We sued the Biden Department of Labor to stop a rule that would let 401(k) managers direct funds toward ESG investments and fought the SEC's proposals to mandate ESG disclosures for corporations and investment companies. The Department of Labor's other proposals to require ESG considerations in retirement investments also met with our strong opposition, as did moves by the FDIC, the Office of the Comptroller of the Currency, and the Municipal Securities Rulemaking Board to impose ESG-based reporting and standards.

Republican Attorneys General made it clear: We wouldn't stand by as these private and federal forces tried to push their ideological agendas on American workers and retirees. We fought to protect Americans' investments from being weaponized by the Net-Zero Alliance and their allies, all in the name of preserving the free market. One of the most pointed challenges to ESG's overreach came in a powerful letter led by Alabama Attorney General Steve Marshall, then–Utah Attorney General Sean Reyes, and the rest of us Republican Attorneys General. We addressed our concerns directly to major asset managers, warning that ESG-focused strategies posed significant risks to both fiduciary duty and economic freedom. In the letter, we wrote, "Americans deserve investment strategies that are driven by financial interests, not political agendas." We emphasized the harm in using Americans' retirement and pension funds to "advance woke ESG goals, often without transparency or consent," calling these practices a betrayal of the purpose of investment. ESG's goals, we argued, were "incompatible with fiduciary duty" and fundamentally "threaten the very foundation of economic freedom." In no uncertain terms, the letter highlighted the risks to American prosperity and independence, underscoring that this was more than just a policy issue—it was a fight to preserve the rights and resources of American workers and retirees.

As Attorney General, I took on ESG directly, exposing its anticapitalist nature and how it was undermining the prosperity of hardworking Americans by prioritizing ideology over financial well-being. It became clear to me that this agenda was not just harmful but fundamentally rooted in a worldview that robbed retirees of their hard-earned pensions and compromised the American way of life. ESG was pushing radical policies that favored the politically connected and the powerful over everyday people.

Recognizing the sweeping influence of the Net-Zero Alliance, I led a first-of-its-kind investigation into the six largest U.S. banks involved, which held nearly 40 percent of the country's banking assets. This alliance's commitment to net-zero emissions wasn't just rhetoric—it translated into active targeting of sectors like manufacturing and fossil fuels, threatening jobs and economic stability. Our investigation sought to hold these financial giants accountable, ensuring they wouldn't use their power to drive a radical agenda at the expense of our economy and workers. All of the banks pulled out of the alliance, just as Joe Biden was leaving office, saying they would continue working on their commitments independently.

Protecting Missouri's workers, retirees, and businesses from the overreach of multinational corporations and global elites was my duty—and I wasn't going to back down. The ESG movement and its various forms should be stopped cold, and a game plan can be executed to expose climate alarmists for what they are. The whole Net-Zero movement seeks to tell folks what they can't have, all while John Kerry flies around on a private jet. The only way the climate alarmists get to where they want to go is to take drastic measures, including denying credit-worthy applicants—like farmers—simply for using diesel trucks on their property. And the irony is, none of it will make an ounce of difference to the climate. It is utter insanity. The efforts we've taken are working.

But this only happens if we have the courage to fight back. There is still much to do on this front, and I believe the United States Congress is the place to do it. Since taking office, I have introduced legislation aimed at curbing the influence of ESG policies in our financial system, starting with a bill to block federal agencies from enforcing ESG-related mandates on private businesses. This includes proposals to limit the power of asset managers with fiduciary duties to their investors who attempt to impose ideological investment standards on Americans' pensions and retirement funds.

I've also pushed for stricter oversight of the SEC's attempts to weave ESG into disclosure requirements, ensuring that corporations aren't compelled to disclose so-called "climate risks" or social metrics that have no bearing on their financial performance. Additionally, I've worked with fellow lawmakers to sponsor a bill that would protect credit access for industries targeted by ESG—such as agriculture and fossil fuels—preventing banks from denying financing based on ideological grounds rather than financial viability. Moreover, more needs to be done to eliminate all forms of woke "debanking" practices outlined by many, including veteran investor Marc Andreessen in his epic podcast with Joe Rogan in late November 2024.

Through these efforts and the executive actions by President Trump, we're setting the stage to dismantle the ESG framework that has been used to pressure American businesses into compliance with a political agenda. It's a fight for transparency, for accountability, and ultimately, for the rights of American workers and consumers to operate in a marketplace unshackled by the whims of woke warriors, climate alarmists and corporate elites.

But the fight is not over.

Part VII

The End Game

Chapter 18

PLAYING TO WIN

In the fall of 2024, I spent a great deal of time traveling the country with President Trump and my friend and fellow Senate freshman JD Vance. More than once, I climbed aboard "Trump Force One," the well-appointed Boeing 757 that carried President Trump and his team to rallies all over the country. During the closing weekend of the campaign on November 1, 2024, I had settled into my seat across from where President Trump would later sit when another guest arrived. It was Robert F. Kennedy Jr., a man who was still several weeks away from being nominated as President Trump's Secretary of Health and Human Services.

It had been a few years since our paths had crossed at that RAGA conference in Utah. I wasn't sure he would remember me. He did. He told me that he still appreciated everything I'd done in Missouri to hold back the Biden Administration during the Covid-19 pandemic. I told him I appreciated him as well. He also thanked me for the work I had done to pull back the curtain on the vast censorship enterprise perpetrated by the Biden regime on the American people. It's been quite a journey for the both of us since meeting in Utah three years earlier. The world had turned over a few times, and I consider him a friend, especially after we bonded during our travels over our favorite *Curb Your Enthusiasm* episodes—his wife, Cheryl Hines, costarred with Larry David on the show.

Looking back on things now, I can see Kennedy was exactly right. Although it might seem that the relationship between Big Tech and

the Biden Administration was always clear, in fact the vast majority of the collusion was conducted in secret, and there wasn't much
public evidence of that at the time. Revealing the extent of the vast
censorship enterprise took thousands of hours of work, digging
and suing. And if it weren't for our work and then Elon Musk buying Twitter—and the subsequent release of the Twitter Files, which
led to the House investigation—all of that collusion and censorship
would still be labeled a "conspiracy theory." Moreover, our work
took conviction and a team of dedicated people who knew where
to look, what buttons to push, and what strategies to use—and
never taking no for an answer. If it hadn't been for our deposition
of Elvis Chan, the world *might* never have learned about the extent
to which the FBI was protecting the Biden family at the expense
of the American people. If it hadn't been for our careful research
into the nature of the relationship between the White House and
Meta, among other social media companies, we might never have
seen a blatant admission from Mark Zuckerberg that he'd engaged
in censorship. In hindsight, our willingness to take this fight on before
anyone else led to the unveiling of an Orwellian scheme to silence the
American people on a scale never seen before. By revealing the truth,
we've now seen a resurgence and a revitalized commitment to free
speech in America.

If we hadn't stood up against the vaccine mandate and won at the
Supreme Court, the Covid tyranny would have raged on, devouring
livelihoods and individual liberty on a massive scale. If we hadn't
stood up to the student loan debt forgiveness scheme and won at the
Supreme Court, American taxpayers would have been on the hook
for another half a trillion dollars. If we wouldn't have exposed the
woke ideology in our schools, the American people wouldn't have
had that issue on the ballot to reject.

History will show the first two years of the Biden Administration
brought the most aggressively liberal, authoritarian, and antiliberty

excesses of government that America has ever seen. President Trump promised to undo them and move an agenda that resonated with the great working class of America and our hopes and dreams for the future. My role, as it turned out, was to hold the line long enough for the cavalry to arrive. On November 5, the cavalry arrived, and the American people delivered President Trump a clear mandate.

Along the way, in different instances and elections, the American people also provided their own verdict on the cases we brought in court. The fights were many, and as each front opened up, our battles may have seemed like isolated wins here or there. But now they provide a comprehensive playbook on how to fight back against the Left and win. We filed a lawsuit against the People's Republic of China, crafting it in such a way that it has survived many challenges in court. We fought back against the Left's excesses during Covid-19, demonstrating how the court system could be used to curb the authority of the federal government. We did our part to secure the border, defend the right to bear arms, and ensure that the material being taught to our children in schools wasn't rooted in radical cultural Marxism. Over the course of the two years that we carried on these fights, we received plenty of criticism from the media. It seemed that every other day, some news organization printed a story assailing our actions as "frivolous" or worse.

Fortunately, we knew the people had our back—not just the ones in Missouri, but all over the country. When things got tough, I always turned to the messages that rolled in through our portal, sifting through the junk and hate to find testimonials from parents whose children we'd helped and students who were able to stay in school because of the actions we'd taken. These people, I knew, were being told every day that failing to adhere to the latest woke fad was tantamount to treason or some sort of "ism." Joe Biden and Kamala Harris had told them that being proud of the United States of America made them fascists. Their accounts on social media were blocked and shadow banned. Their kids were learning that this country was nothing but a racist colonial project where white supremacy was still the order of the day. There were days when it seemed like the soft tyranny imposed by Joe Biden and his Democratic backers would win out.

As it turned out, though, a government can't alienate more than half the population of a country for very long—at least not without a serious backlash. And on November 5, 2024, after a long and strange campaign, a backlash is exactly what the Democrats got. Despite their attempts to frame the election as yet another Emergency™ and that Trump and half of America were a Threat to Democracy™, the American people saw through it; the American people sat in their jury box and saw the excesses of government; they saw the lawfare; they saw the slow-moving disaster that was the Biden-Harris years and rendered their verdict. The American people showed up in record numbers to send Donald Trump back to the White House. The American people showed that they would not be silenced, and we are already seeing a resurgence of patriotism.

But the Left is not going to go quietly. Compared to what's coming, the efforts of the Resistance™ to stop President Trump's agenda are going to seem mild. Given the fact that Democrats have little to no power in Congress, they are going to crack open their playbook and go at us with renewed vigor. Lawsuits have arrived, and more will come. So have challenges to almost every single one of President Trump's executive orders. Phony declarations of a "constitutional crisis," and statements such as "democracy is under attack" are going to come down every day, and the legacy media—which appears to have learned nothing from President Trump's landslide victory—will repeat them.

Their tired playbook is also set for the next "emergency." Whether it's a "climate emergency" or "crisis" (with "record-breaking heat" now a constant refrain), the drumbeat has begun. We're hearing "The

world is hotter on this day than any other day in recorded history."
Maybe it's a return to masks or Covid lockdowns with a new vari-
ant or virus. Maybe it'll just be Trump himself. Whatever form this
takes, the tactics of the Left are set: Create the emergency, scapegoat
anyone who questions, dehumanize them, aggregate power, and
exercise that power to silence dissent. Just as the unvaccinated became a target of hate, the Left will continue to mobilize hate against
those who oppose its crazy excesses. Look no further than the hate
directed at Elon Musk and the firebombing of Tesla dealerships, all
because he dared to make government more efficient and expose so
much grift.

How do we stop this kind of tyranny from ever happening again?
The answer lies in dismantling the Administrative State and restoring accountability at every level of government. We must draw clear
lines ensuring that no health authority, agency, or global organization can ever use a crisis to circumvent the will of the people. The
days of unaccountable bureaucrats, rogue agencies, and their arbitrary policies should be consigned to the ash heap of history.

We also need a full-scale push to untangle the unholy alliance
between Big Tech and Big Government. Some Big Tech leaders are
saying all the right things now. Maybe they have been "red-pilled" or
maybe they are just saying what's expedient, but we have to ensure
what happened never happens again. So, we should make individual
bureaucrats personally liable to citizens if they violate that citizen's
First Amendment Rights and if Big Tech platforms work to silence
speech in a way that makes them a publisher not a platform, they
should lose Section 230 protections. We must be willing to take on
the global NGO nexus that promotes mass migration and censorship. The Censorship Industrial Complex must be dismantled to
preserve our fundamental rights. Freedom and liberty are still in the
crosshairs of those who seek to limit them. Covid was the trial run;
their next "crisis" will be used to further consolidate power. There

are certainly more ideas out there, but we know their tactics now. And we have our own playbook, one grounded in the values of the American republic.

We also know that we can beat them in court. From the moment President Trump took office in January of 2025, liberal activists have sought to tie him up using the old playbook. At the district court level, they might obtain some temporary wins. But as they make their way up through the court system, these efforts will largely be seen as what they are: deliberate attempts to nullify the election of President Trump through lawfare; efforts to inhibit core Article II powers, preserve Biden-era overreach, or push policies that would never be supported legislatively or by the American people.

As I said in the prologue, there are also key differences between what we did during Joe Biden's four years in office and what the Left is doing now. Our lawsuits sought to restore individual liberty, defend the rule of law, fight for everyday Americans against the massive power of the federal government, and prevent government overreach. In contrast, Democrat lawsuits aim to preserve the expansion of government power at the *expense* of individual freedom and the rule of law.

Other market forces are working to our advantage as well. With distrust of the legacy media at all-time highs and social media censorship seemingly in retreat, information is becoming more diffused and the liberal middlemen used to having control are losing it. Literally and figuratively. This is a positive development.

As Attorney General of Missouri, I didn't just talk about the abuses of Covid tyranny, or an unlawful student debt forgiveness power grab, or the collectivist ESG movement, or suppression of speech—I took action. I stood in the arena and fought back. I sued China for unleashing the coronavirus and won; sued the federal government for forcing vaccine mandates on Americans and won; sued the federal government for mandating a vaccine for kids enrolled in Head

Start and won; sued cities and counties for mask mandates and won; sued school districts for the forced masking of kids and won; took on Biden's open borders policy and won (for a while); took on ESG and woke corporate overlords and won; sued the Biden Administration for unlawfully canceling student loan debt and won; took on CRT in our schools; and sued the Biden Administration for colluding with some of the most powerful companies the world has ever known to create a vast censorship enterprise in the most important free speech case in American history. These weren't just wins for Missouri but indeed for every American who believes in freedom.

Freedom and liberty are under constant assault by the Left and further action is needed to protect our God-given rights.

We must fight for accountability and against arbitrary rules that threaten our core liberties. We must protect fundamental free speech and expression of dissent. These are our principles we arm ourselves with for the fights ahead.

We now face the broader battle in a new era, armed with the lessons we've learned and the successes we've achieved. Our efforts against the Biden Administration and its excesses held the damn from busting. The American people saw those excesses and delivered their own verdict and a mandate on November 5, 2004, and sent President Trump back to Washington to disrupt the Establishment.

The next fights with the Left and their movement to upend America won't necessarily look the same on the surface, but we now come to the new fight with valuable lessons learned and big wins under our belt, and finally moving our agenda forward will take courage. We did it in Missouri; now we can do it across (and for) America. Stopping them will take courage, but we have the tools, the experience, and, most importantly, the support of the people.

At the conclusion of the Constitutional Convention in 1787, Benjamin Franklin was famously asked what sort of government the delegates had created. He replied, "A republic, if you can keep it."

The future of this republic is in our hands. The task ahead demands vigilance, action, and an unwavering commitment to the principles upon which this nation was founded. The path is clear—let's rise to the occasion and preserve the promise of America for generations to come.

EPILOGUE

When I was growing up, my dad got one week of vacation a year. More than a few times our family would make our way to Silver Dollar City in Branson, Missouri. We'd make the four-hour trek from St. Louis to Branson on Interstate 44, then state highway 65. We'd stay in a motel somewhere on the Branson "strip" and spend a day at a water park and at least a day at the theme park. In addition to the roller coasters and other rides at Silver Dollar City, the sprawling theme park was like going back in time. Everyone who worked in the park was dressed like people in the Ozarks would have dressed in the nineteenth century. The women who worked there would weave their baskets and you could buy handmade knickknacks or wreaths but it was the craftsmen there who would grab my attention—especially the blacksmiths. Maybe there was some ancestral pull to it all, as the surname Schmitt was likely derived from the word for "blacksmith" in Germany, but the more likely explanation is that I was a kid and thought it was cool. There was just something fascinating about witnessing the forging process—the shaping of something strong through pressure and heat.

Writing this book required me to look back at a time that was wild, unique, and consequential, what role I played in it, and how I was forged by it.

When I was sworn in as Missouri's forty-third Attorney General in early 2019, I had no idea what was in store for me or my team that I would assemble. No one could have known. I had every intention of trying to make the office the best office in the country but obviously couldn't have predicted a once-in-a-lifetime global pandemic and the most radical, power-hungry, and lawless administration in American history lied just months in front of me.

Being on the other side of the fever dream that gripped our country for four years now gives me some perspective. It's a perspective forged by the fights, the wins, the losses, the decision-making, and how standing up for what you believe in is always the right thing to do.

This was a time of forced masking, mass migration, censorship, lawlessness, and lawfare—not somewhere else but here, in America. Somebody had to do something. So, I did.

In writing this book and through a lot of self-reflection on the Why I realized that there have been two real inflection points in my life. The first came when my son was diagnosed with a rare genetic condition called tuberous sclerosis. It causes tubers to grow on different organs, including his brain. Stephen is nonverbal, on the autism spectrum, and has epilepsy. He has seizures almost daily, and when he was just a few years old he had one that lasted four hours. All I could do was hold his hand on that hospital bed and pray. The only *other* thing I could do was watch the minutes and seconds tick by on the red digital clock on the wall as they had to wait twenty minutes before administering a new medication to try and stop the seizures. They had gone through several already and only had one more to give before they might induce a coma. I felt so helpless and completely powerless. The last one they tried worked.

We almost lost Stephen that day. After that, we spent well over a week in the intensive care unit. From that experience I went through a process of discernment about what I really wanted to do with my life. At that point my focus had been practicing law, building my career, and starting a family, but I decided there was something more for me to do, so I ultimately decided that I would run for office and try to make a difference—to have a bigger impact. Stephen was and is my inspiration for all of this. I could have never predicted back then where I'd be now, but what a gift I received from my boy and from God.

St. Ignatius of Loyola wrote a lot about indifference. Indifference isn't not-caring. It's the idea that you can take any situation, even one you don't want or even fear, and you can make the most out of it. This can be hard to do, but once again, Stephen was my teacher. So, this first inflection point got me into politics. The second one sharpened my focus and taught me a lot about leadership, courage, and another big, important Why.

The second inflection point was Covid. As I said earlier, power doesn't necessarily corrupt, but it does reveal. And during Covid, too many people who should have never had power had it and abused it in ways I never could have imagined. It was during this time I decided that enough was enough and someone had to fight back. No more bullies on the bus. The defender-and-protector instinct kicked in—whether by nature or nurture—this was the time. So I pushed my way into the arena and fought. It was through "The Many Fights of Eric Schmitt," as one publication put it, chronicled in this book, that I gained even greater resolve to lead, to not back down when you're fighting for what is right no matter the cost or criticism. It was during this time that a new resolve was forged, one I carry with me to this day.

Perhaps the biggest takeaway from writing this book and the reflection required to do so—aside from my gratitude for my faith and family—is there is a certain pride that can come with taking on the tough fights. But you have to have the courage to step into the arena. Once you do, you realize that what people are looking for more than anything is authentic leadership. Now, to be clear, it's a lot easier to just go along, do the ribbon cuttings, and not rock the boat. The disincentives for truth-telling are many. Taking on the status quo, the Establishment, the powerful, or Settled Science™ will gain you enemies, and you may even lose a few friends. I know I did, but I gained many more, and many friendships were strengthened. I have great peace of mind knowing the fight, the struggle is always worth it. And ... we were right.

In short, it's a lot easier to just go along and not stand out when there are headwinds, and there are many rewards for that—but that's just not me.

Through this forging I gained a great self-knowledge and a greater sense of purpose. I could be a voice for the voiceless—a voice for those like my son; a voice for the parents who were investigated for showing up to school board meetings; a voice for the five-year-old being forced to wear a mask all day long in school; a voice for the family who doesn't want radical CRT infused into their kids' grade school education; a voice for the guy working his tail off who just wanted to not take the Covid shot and keep his job and his ability to feed his family; a voice for the community affected by mass illegal immigration; a voice for the worker who resents being browbeaten at DEI struggle sessions he's forced to attend at work; a voice for the truck driver or the waitress who doesn't feel they should have to pay the student loan debt of the Ivy League theater professor; a voice for a fellow citizen who was expressing a dissenting viewpoint censored by her government and Big Tech behemoths.

This greater sense of purpose, born from the catalytic experiences with my son and forged by a pandemic, social unrest, and an overreaching federal government, was to fight for the little guy and those who need a champion. I am proud to have stood in the breach and to be a last line of defense for the freedoms we hold dear in a country that I absolutely love. Thank you for reading. I am grateful. AMDG

ACKNOWLEDGMENTS

Any thanks begin with my wife, Jaime. I am incredibly grateful for her love and patience. To my wonderful kids, Stephen, Sophia, and Olivia: I love you more than any words on any page could ever express. You inspire me every day. I am also thankful for my parents, Steve and Kathy Schmitt, for their consistent encouragement throughout my life, and for my sisters, Christy and Stephanie, for being two wonderful younger sisters. I am also blessed to have a great extended family of aunts, uncles, cousins, and in-laws.

Thank you to the amazing team we assembled in the Missouri Attorney General's Office who fought alongside me in some of the most consequential legal battles in a generation, including but not limited to John Sauer, Justin Smith, Cris Stevens, Tom Albus, Marianna Deal, Chris Nuelle, Megan Werdehausen, Morgan Corder, Drew Dzeidzic, Michael Talent, Jesus Osete, Charlie Capps, Jeremiah Morgan, Ken Capps, Maria Lanahan, Alyssa Mayer, Jason Lewis, Jonathan Hensley, Josh Foster, Josh Seyer, Chris Wray, Zack Bluestone, Maddie Green, Diana Hanes, Julia Rives, Jay Atkins, Doug Dolan, Kerry Kroll, Kiley Williams, Maddie Siren, Patrick Flesch, Rhonda Meyer, Sarah Jones, Shaun Mackelprang, Terry Brady, Todd Scott, Christine Krug, Greg Goodwin, and all the other attorneys and staff who gave it their all to make our office the best in the country.

I am also grateful for meaningful partnerships with former U.S. Attorneys Jeff Jensen and Tim Garrison.

Thanks to the many folks in Republican Attorney General world including Jonathan Bunch, Pete Bisbee, Adam Piper, David Johnson, Johnny Koremenos, and all the work America First Legal did led by Stephen Miller. To the many other Attorneys General I had the pleasure to work with, especially those I served with on the Republican Attorneys General Association Executive Board, including Steve Marshall, Alan Wilson, Ken Paxton, Sean Reyes, Ashley Moody, Daniel Cameron, Jeff Landry, Leslie Rutledge, Lynn Fitch, Derek Schmidt, Doug Peterson, and others—thank you as well.

I'd like to thank Keith Urbahn and Dylan Colligan at Javelin for their help in this effort, Eric Nelson at Harper for the opportunity to tell this story, and Sean McGowan for his stellar editorial assistance on this project.

And most importantly, Ad Majorem Dei Gloriam.

NOTES

CHAPTER 1: ATTACK OF THE "EXPERTS"

1. https://www.washingtonpost.com/politics/interactive/2021/tony-fauci-emails/.
2. Jon Miltimore, "The Behavioral Experiment That Helps Explain the Fall of Elizabeth Holmes—and the Horrors of Socialism," FEE.org, January 6, 2022, https://fee.org/articles/the-behavioral-experiment-that-helps-explain-the-fall-of-elizabeth-holmes-and-the-horrors-of-socialism/.
3. https://www.cnn.com/2020/06/05/health/health-care-open-letter-protests-coronavirus-trnd/index.html.
4. Lawrence Wright, *The Plague Year: America in the Time of Covid* (New York: Knopf, 2021), 9.
5. Wright, *The Plague Year*, 13.

CHAPTER 2: SCHMITT V. THE PEOPLE'S REPUBLIC OF CHINA

1. https://www.globaltimes.cn/content/1188309.shtml.

CHAPTER 3: THE LEFT'S DARK MONEY V. THE VOTERS

1. https://x.com/kenvogel/status/922955410327425027?s=20.
2. https://www.newyorker.com/news/persons-of-interest/the-first-defense-against-trumps-assault-on-democracy.
3. https://www.wsj.com/articles/zuckerbucks-shouldnt-pay-for-elections-mark-zuckerberg-center-for-technology-and-civic-life-trump-biden-2020-11640912907.
4. https://www.wsj.com/articles/zuckerbucks-shouldnt-pay-for-elections-mark-zuckerberg-center-for-technology-and-civic-life-trump-biden-2020-11640912907.
5. https://www.nytimes.com/2022/01/29/us/politics/democrats-dark-money-donors.html.
6. https://www.pewresearch.org/politics/2022/10/31/views-of-election-administration-and-confidence-in-vote-counts/.
7. https://www.pewresearch.org/politics/2022/10/31/views-of-election-administration-and-confidence-in-vote-counts/.
8. https://x.com/OversightPR/status/1838294902506983735.
9. https://www.heritage.org/election-integrity/commentary/illegal-aliens-are-still-voting-our-elections.

CHAPTER 5: THE LIBERATION GAME

1. https://x.com/GovParsonMO/status/1466539935750508547.

CHAPTER 6: MASK MANDATES IN LOCAL SCHOOLS
1. David McCollough, *Truman* (New York: Simon & Schuster, 1992), 16.
2. https://www.columbiamissourian.com/news/k12_education/columbia-public
    -schools-will-require-masks-to-be-worn-inside/article_a0aa5b04-fc7a-11eb-a1e7
    -87e1ee3e90d8.html.

CHAPTER 7: *MISSOURI V. BIDEN*: THE MOST IMPORTANT FREE SPEECH
CASE IN AMERICAN HISTORY
1. https://constitutioncenter.org/the-constitution/supreme-court-case-library/west
    -virginia-board-of-education-v-barnette.
2. https://scholar.google.com/scholar_case?case=2597159087908243157&q
    =Biden&hl=en&as_sdt=4,60&as_ylo=2021.

CHAPTER 8: MISSOURI, TEXAS V. BIDEN: HOLDING BACK THE FLOOD
1. https://thehill.com/blogs/blog-briefing-room/news/452846-harris-meghan
    -mccain-spar-over-decriminalization-of-border/.
2. https://freebeacon.com/biden-administration/flashback-biden-tells-migrants-to
    -surge-to-the-border/.
3. https://x.com/JoeBiden/status/1237893066981117956?s=20.
4. https://www.npr.org/sections/president-biden-takes-office/2021/01/21
    /959074750/biden-suspends-deportations-stops-remain-in-mexico-policy.
5. https://www.supremecourt.gov/DocketPDF/19/19A960/137535
    /20200309155332028_2020.03.09%20op%20stay%20remain%20in
    %20mexico%20FINAL.pdf.

CHAPTER 9: MISSOURI, TEXAS V. BIDEN PART II: BUILD THE DAMN WALL
1. Jeffrey Toobin, *The Oath: The Obama White House and the Supreme Court*
    (New York: Doubleday, 2012), 25.

CHAPTER 10: FIGHTING FOR TITLE 42
1. https://www.cnn.com/2022/01/19/politics/title-42-biden/index.html.
2. https://www.azag.gov/sites/default/files/docs/press-releases/2022/complaints
    /1-Complaint.pdf.
3. https://www.texastribune.org/2022/05/20/title-42-border-judge-ruling-migrants/.

CHAPTER 11: CHIPPING AWAY
1. https://www.heritage.org/political-process/report/woodrow-wilson-godfather
    -liberalism.
2. https://www.heritage.org/political-process/report/woodrow-wilson-godfather
    -liberalism.
3. https://www.nationalaffairs.com/publications/detail/confronting-the
    -administrative-state.

CHAPTER 12: THE CASE I ALWAYS WANTED
1. https://www.wsj.com/articles/taxation-by-citation-undermines-trust-between
    -cops-and-citizens-1438987412.
2. https://www.thecentersquare.com/missouri/attorney-general-sues-small-missouri
    -town-for-taxation-by-traffic-citation/article_41acdba8-4979-11ec-8ec2
    -13150c28f698.html.

CHAPTER 14: STICKING TO OUR GUNS
1. Antonin Scalia, *The Essential Scalia: On the Constitution, the Courts, and the Rule of
    Law,* ed. Jeffrey S. Sutton and Edward Whelan (New York: Crown Forum, 2020), 137.

CHAPTER 16: CRT, DEI, AND WHEN PARENTS WERE THE ENEMY
1. https://x.com/Eric_Schmitt/status/1534590071785066499.
2. https://x.com/Eric_Schmitt/status/1534588472031338497.
3. https://www.youtube.com/watch?v=m66rcHzWaPU.

ABOUT THE AUTHOR

Eric Schmitt grew up in a working-class neighborhood and was the first person in his family to attend college out of high school. He is a tireless advocate for the Constitution, individual liberty, and working families. He is a sixth-generation Missourian and currently represents the people of Missouri in the United States Senate. He previously served as his state's Attorney General. He is a member of the Armed Services Committee; the Commerce, Science and Transportation Committee; the Judiciary Committee; and the Joint Economic Committee. He resides in the St. Louis area with his wife, Jaime, and three children, Stephen, Sophia, and Olivia.